Tsuda Umeko

A Gender History of Science and University in Japan

Tsuda Umeko

A Gender History of Science and University in Japan

Yasu Furukawa

TRANS
PACIFIC
PRESS

Tsuda Umeko: A Gender History of Science and University in Japan
Translated from the first Japanese edition of *Tsuda Umeko: Kagaku eno michi, daigaku no yume*
[Tsuda Umeko: The Road to Science and Dream of Founding a University]
Published in 2022 by Tokyo Daigaku Shuppankai.

Published in 2026 by Trans Pacific Press Co., Ltd.

Trans Pacific Press Co., Ltd.
[Editorial Office]
2-2-15-2F, Hamamatsu-cho, Minato-ku,
Tokyo, 1050013, JAPAN
[Registered Office]
PO Box 8547 #19682
Boston, MA, 02114, United States
Email: info@transpacificpress.com
Web: http://www.transpacificpress.com

Copyedited by Dr. Karl E. Smith, Melbourne, Australia
Layout designed and set by Ryo Kuroda, Yokohama, Kanagawa, Japan

Distributors

World
Independent Publishers Group (IPG)
814 N. Franklin Street,
Chicago, IL 60610, USA
Email: frontdesk@ipgbook.com
Web: http://www.ipgbook.com

China
China Publishers Services Ltd.
718, 7/F., Fortune Commercial Building,
362 Sha Tsui Road, Tsuen Wan, N.T.
Hong Kong
Email: edwin@cps-hk.com

Japan
MHM Limited
3-2-3F, Kanda-Ogawamachi, Chiyoda-ku,
Tokyo 101-0052
Email: sales@mhmlimited.co.jp
Web: http://www.mhmlimited.co.jp

Southeast Asia
Alkem Company Pte Ltd.
1, Sunview Road #01-27,
Eco-Tech@Sunview
Singapore 627615
Email: enquiry@alkem.com.sg

ISBN 978-1-920850-57-9 (paperback)
ISBN 978-1-920850-58-6 (eBook)

Front cover: Tsuda Umeko, 1892, and Umeko's manuscript.
Courtesy Tsuda University Archives
Back cover: Laboratory work in the Kosetsu Chemistry Hall, Japan Women's University.
Courtesy Naruse Memorial Hall, Japan Women's University

Contents

About the Author vi
General Notes vii
List of Figures viii
List of Tables x
Acknowledgements 1
Prologue 5

Chapter 1: A Young Japanese Girl in America 13
- Tsuda Sen and Agriculture 14
- Japanese Girls in America 21
- An English Teacher at Peeresses' School 30
- Realizing the Dream of Studying in America Again 36

Chapter 2: Bryn Mawr College and Biology 45
- Department of Biology at Bryn Mawr College 46
- Umeko at Bryn Mawr 56

Chapter 3: Becoming a Biologist 67
- A Summer in Woods Hole 68
- Research with Morgan 71
- Struggles and Return Home 79
- Farewell to Biology 88

Chapter 4: Behind the Scenes at Joshi Eigaku Juku 93
- Arguments against Higher Education for Women 95
- Enthusiastic "Dojo (Little Girl)" 100
- Days of Farewell 110

Chapter 5: From Juku to Daigaku 117
- Hoshino Ai and Her Study at Bryn Mawr 118
- Creating the Science Department during the War 128
- Toward a "True Daigaku" 142

Epilogue 151
Bibliography 167
Map of the Eastern United States 194
Index 195

About the Author

Born in Japan in 1948, Furukawa Yasu obtained a Bachelor of Engineering degree from the Tokyo Institute of Technology. He received a Ph.D. in the History of Science from the University of Oklahoma in the United States in 1983. He held the position of Professor of History of Science at Tokyo Denki University and then at Nihon University. He served as president of the Japanese Society for the History of Chemistry from 2011 to 2016. Currently, he is a visiting fellow at the Graduate University for Advanced Studies (SOKENDAI), Japan. In 2018, he was awarded the John and Martha Morris Award from the Society for the History of Alchemy and Chemistry in the UK. In 2022 he received the Mainichi Publishing Culture Award, and in 2024 the History of Science Society of Japan's Special Award. He is the author of *Inventing Polymer Science: Staudinger, Carothers, and the Emergence of Macromolecular Chemistry* (Philadelphia: University of Pennsylvania Press, 1998); *Kagaku no shakai-shi: Runessansu kara 20 seiki made* [A Social History of Science: From the Renaissance to the 20th Century] (Tokyo: Nansosha, 1989; pocket book edition, Tokyo: Chikuma Shobo, 2018); and *Kagaku-sha tachi no Kyoto gakuha: Kita Gen-itsu to Nihon no kagaku* [Chemists' Kyoto School: Kita Gen-itsu and Japan's Chemistry] (Kyoto: Kyoto Daigaku Gakujutsu Shuppankai, 2017).

General Notes

(1) This book follows the standard conventions for Japanese names used in scholarly English-language publications on Japan: family names are presented before personal names (e.g., Furukawa Yasu). For the convenience of librarians, booksellers, and to facilitate distribution, the author's name is listed in Western order on the cover and title page (Yasu Furukawa).

(2) The romanization of Japanese words and names basically follows the Hepburn system.

(3) Umeko's original given name was "Mume," but she used "Umeko" when she was employed as a teacher at the Peeresses' School. While in the United States, she favored the name "Ume" or "Umé." She officially adopted the name "Umeko" in her family register in November 1902, and is referred to as "Umeko" throughout this book for the sake of convenience. In Japan, the use of the given name, Umeko, rather than the surname, Tsuda, is more common when referring to Tsuda Umeko. This book adheres to that convention.

(4) In Japanese, *daigaku* is the common word for both college and university. The official English name of Tsuda Juku Daigaku is currently "Tsuda University." It was referred to as "Tsuda College" from its inception in 1948 until 2017 (when it had two faculties). In this book, the term "Tsuda College" is used, unless it refers to today's Tsuda Juku Daigaku.

List of Figures

Figure 1.1 Tsuda Sen at the 1873 Vienna World's Fair 16
Figure 1.2 Tsuda Sen, *Nogyo Sanji* 17
Figure 1.3 Tsuda Sen at Gakunosha Agricultural School 20
Figure 1.4 Five female students, 1872 25
Figure 1.5 Umeko at age 7 28
Figure 1.6 Umeko at around age 11 in 1876 28
Figure 1.7 The three students at the World's Fair in Philadelphia, Summer 1876 28
Figure 1.8 Yamakawa Sutematsu, Vassar College, 1882 29
Figure 1.9 Umeko aged around 18, ca. 1883 31
Figure 1.10 The opening ceremony at the Peeresses' School, 1885 35
Figure 1.11 Tsuda Umeko and her family, 1886 35
Figure 1.12 Adeline Dodge Lanman, Umeko's foster mother in the USA 37
Figure 1.13 Umeko's "Application for Resignation," April 30, 1889 41
Figure 1.14 Umeko's official application to study abroad, May 9, 1889 41

Figure 2.1 Aerial View of the Bryn Mawr College campus, ca. 1890s 47
Figure 2.2 Martha Carey Thomas, 1889 49
Figure 2.3 Edmund Beecher Wilson, ca. 1890 52
Figure 2.4 Taylor Hall, 1890s 53
Figure 2.5 Biology Laboratory (Taylor Hall, 3rd floor), 1886 53
Figure 2.6 Biology Laboratory (Taylor Hall, 3rd floor), ca. 1890 54
Figure 2.7 Library (Taylor Hall, 1st floor), ca. 1890 54
Figure 2.8 Umeko in a gown, 1889 59
Figure 2.9 Umeko in the dormitory with Anna Powers, 1890 60
Figure 2.10 Umeko's "Application for Extension of Study," June 15, 1891 64

Figure 3.1 Woods Hole Marine Biological Laboratory facilities, c.1890 69
Figure 3.2 The faculty and students of the 1891 summer course 69
Figure 3.3 Practical training scene, 1895 70
Figure 3.4 Practical training scene, 1896 70
Figure 3.5 Thomas Hunt Morgan, 1891 73
Figure 3.6 Morgan on the Bryn Mawr College campus, 1898 73
Figure 3.7 Umeko's manuscript for the paper 76

Figure 3.8 Paper with Morgan, "The Orientation of the Frog's Egg," 1894 76
Figure 3.9 Ida Henrietta Hyde 78
Figure 3.10 Umeko in her Bryn Mawr days, age 24 78
Figure 3.11 Mitsukuri Kakichi 85

Figure 4.1 Yamakawa Kenjiro 96
Figure 4.2 Hiratsuka Raicho, 1910 98
Figure 4.3 At the opening of Joshi Eigaku Juku in 1900 101
Figure 4.4 Umeko, 1901 102
Figure 4.5 The library of Joshi Eigaku Juku, Goban-cho Campus 103
Figure 4.6 Nitobe Inazo, 1902 104
Figure 4.7 Yamakawa Kikue, 1920 105
Figure 4.8 Umeko in her later years, 1927 113

Figure 5.1 Bryn Mawr College, graduating class of 1912 123
Figure 5.2 Joshi Eigaku Juku, October 3, 1924, when Umeko visited from her sickbed 126
Figure 5.3 Hoshino Ai at the time of her appointment as acting principal 126
Figure 5.4 The new school building in Kodaira, shortly after completion 127
Figure 5.5 Kuwaki Ayao with Albert Einstein and his wife at Kyushu Imperial University, December 1922 138
Figure 5.6 Students working in a munitions factory on campus, 1944 140
Figure 5.7 Hoshino Ai and first-year science students at graduation in 1947 140
Figure 5.8 Laboratory work in the science department of Tsuda Juku shortly after the war 141
Figure 5.9 A science student using a balance-scale for weighing, shortly after the war 141
Figure 5.10 Hoshino Ai, the first president of Tsuda College at the Kodaira Campus, March 1951 147

Figure Epilogue 1 Yasui Kono, 1927 155
Figure Epilogue 2 Laboratory work at the School of Home Economics in the Kosetsu Chemistry Hall at Japan Women's University 158
Figure Epilogue 3 Tange Ume conducting an experiment at RIKEN 159

List of Tables

Table 2.1 Biology Faculty of Bryn Mawr College 55
Table 2.2 Courses Tsuda Umeko took (1889–1892) 58

Table 3.1 Course Enrollment in the Department of Biology at Bryn Mawr College 77

Acknowledgements

This research grew out of my personal interest in the relationship between Tsuda Umeko and biology, an interest that first emerged during my stay in Philadelphia. As a historian of science, I was particularly drawn to the theme of this study, which explores the meaning and significance of "doing science" and "having done science" across two cultures separated by the Pacific Ocean, as experienced by a Japanese woman teaching English during the turbulent Meiji era. It was a natural progression for my inquiry to expand beyond Umeko's individual career to encompass the educational and research systems of her time, as well as the gender-related issues embedded within them. This is a topic to which I have long been committed, and I believe I have ultimately achieved my purpose. Although there are several points I might have treated in greater detail, I am nonetheless pleased to have brought this project to completion and to present this book. Despite the academic nature of this monograph, I have sought to make it accessible to a general readership. It would give me great satisfaction if any part of this work were to prove of interest to its readers.

I would like to take this opportunity to express my deep gratitude to my mentor, Mary Jo Nye, who guided me into the fascinating world of history of science scholarship since I was a graduate student at the University of Oklahoma. She has always supported me and offered invaluable advice. I am also grateful to my classmate and friend, Liba Taub; it has been a privilege to study the history of science alongside her.

It is a pleasure to thank all the people who provided invaluable assistance in the course of my research on Tsuda Umeko, particularly in examining primary sources at the following institutions: Tsuda University Archives, Tsuda Family Collection, Gakushuin Archives, Imperial Household Archives, National Diet Library in Japan, Toho University Nukada Memorial Archives, Ochanomizu University Historical Museum, Naruse Memorial Hall at Japan Women's University, Yamakawa Kikue Memorial Association, Nitobe Memorial Museum, Kyushu University Archives, The Graduate University for Advanced Studies (SOKENDAI) Library, University of Tokyo Komaba Library, Kawasaki City Library, Bryn Mawr College Special Collections, Woods Hole Marine Biological Laboratory Library, Archives and Special Collections at Vassar College Library, State University of New York, Oswego, Penfield Library Special Collections, and American Association of University Women Washington (DC) Archives.

The completion of this book would not have been possible without the cooperation of numerous individuals. I would like to express my profound gratitude to (listed alphabetically) Akiyama Michihiko, Homei Aya, Iino Masako, Ito Kenji, Iwama Yukina, Kawashima Keiko, Koretsune Karin, Harald Kümmerle, Kuroda Kotaro, Mizoguchi Hajime, Mizushima Nozomi, Nagashima Kentaro, Nakada Yuki, Nakahara Lisa, Nakane Michiyo, Ogawa Mariko, Okumura Naofumi, Sumida Tomohisa, Takahashi Yuko, Takuwa Yoshimi, Tsuda Mamoru, Tsuda Michio, Yajima Michiko, Yamada Yuka, Yamamoto Mihoko, and Yatsumimi Toshifumi for their invaluable contributions, which included useful information, comments, suggestions, and encouragement. Furthermore, I have derived intellectual stimulation on this theme from my classes in the Department of History and Philosophy of Science at the University of Tokyo (Komaba campus), as well as from discussions in the Hayama Seminar on History of Science and Science Studies and in the "Systematic Study on the Emergence of Women Scientists in Japan" group meetings supported by a JSPS (Japan Society for the Promotion of Sciences) Grant-in-aid for Science Research (C) 20K00267. The translation of the original text and its production was financially supported by a JSPS Grant-in-aid for Science Research for Publication of Scientific Research Results 25HP5044. I would like to thank Komatsu Mika of Tokyo Daigaku Shuppankai for her meticulous editing of the original book. Furuya Uematsu Yuko of Trans Pacific Press has provided invaluable support to the English version of the project, for which I am profoundly grateful. Finally, I would like to thank my wife Natsuko for always supporting and encouraging me.

Prologue

> It is well known that Tsuda Umeko-sensei was an English educator in Japan, but few people know that she was also a biologist.
>
> – Nakanishi Fumiko,
> "Something about Tsuda-Sensei," 1929

> While sitting under the [cherry] tree, I made the acquaintance of an old woman who resembled a flower sprite. Thinking back, I realize that she was probably somewhere between fifty and sixty years old, but to a young girl of eighteen, she seemed like a very old lady. She was apparently an alumna of Tsuda who had come to the school on an errand. Like me, she had stopped under the tree to look at the flowers in their glory, and when she noticed that I was a new student, she began to talk to me in a rambling way. "You know, Tsuda-sensei did research on frogs' eggs at a college in America." I knew no such thing about Tsuda Umeko and stared at her blankly.
>
> – Oba Minako,
> *Reflections on Tsuda Umeko*, 2021

Tsuda Umeko (1864–1929) is widely recognized as a pioneer in English education for women in Japan. She is also known as the founder of Joshi Eigaku Juku (Women's School for English Studies), the precursor to the present-day Tsuda Juku Daigaku (Tsuda University), a private institution of higher education for women, located in Tokyo. In the contemporary era, she has gained increased recognition among the Japanese populace due to her depiction on the newly issued 5,000-yen bill. However, the relationship between Umeko and the natural sciences has rarely been discussed, and is not well known.

The present volume is an English translation of my Japanese book, *Tsuda Umeko: Kagaku eno michi, daigaku no yume* [Tsuda Umeko: The Road to Science and Dream of Founding a University], published by Tokyo Daigaku Shuppankai in 2022. The original work offered a new perspective on Tsuda Umeko's life and career, examining them through the lenses of science and gender. Since its publication, it has fortunately attracted considerable attention from a wide range of readers, including scholars, the general public, and the media. The book was honored with the 2022 Mainichi Publishing Culture Award, one of the most prestigious book prizes in Japan. I was also awarded the 2024 Special Award from the History of Science Society of Japan, a testament to the work's academic rigor and contributions to the field. It is with great pleasure that I present this English edition to non-Japanese readers. I have made necessary revisions in the course of translation.

This work is the culmination of research that I began three decades ago. I first encountered Tsuda Umeko in 1992 during a one-year sabbatical from the university in Tokyo where I was employed which allowed me to conduct research at the University of Pennsylvania, located in Philadelphia. My primary objective for this research was to examine the papers of American polymer chemists stored at the Beckman Center for the History of Chemistry (today's Science History Institute), which was then attached to the university.

Through a real estate agent, I arranged to rent an old apartment in Bryn Mawr, a suburban town about 30 minutes from Philadelphia on the Main Line. The apartment was near Bryn Mawr College, a highly regarded institution of higher education for women. The campus, with its picturesque landscape of stately white-stone buildings set amid densely wooded grounds, feels distinctly removed from the bustle of the city. Walking through the campus on weekends soon became a habit of mine.

Along the way, I learned that a Japanese woman named Tsuda Umeko had attended Bryn Mawr a century earlier. One day, driven by curiosity, I visited the archives in the college library where I discovered a meticulously organized file on Tsuda Umeko, complete with her transcripts and correspondence. My interest as a historian of science was quickly deepened when I found that Umeko had studied biology at Bryn Mawr alongside the renowned zoologist Thomas Hunt Morgan.

At a very young age, Umeko was among the first Japanese women to study in the United States, where she resided for nearly eleven years. Upon returning to Japan, she took a job teaching English at the Peeresses' School (Kazoku Jogakko) in Tokyo. In this capacity, she was granted a leave of absence to go to the US again to pursue her studies at Bryn Mawr College, where she majored in biology and demonstrated remarkable academic aptitude. Her teachers commended her aptitude in the biological sciences, and anticipated she would have a promising future as a researcher in this domain. Upon returning to Japan three years later, however, she relinquished her identity as a scientific researcher and dedicated the remainder of her life to teaching English and operating a school for Japanese women.

Why did Umeko study biology in America, and why did she not pursue a scientific career afterwards? The motivation behind her decision intrigued me and I began pursuing answers to these questions. After my sabbatical, I continued to amass material and information on Tsuda Umeko by visiting various archives both in Japan and the United States. This pursuit evolved into a pleasant ancillary project, while I persisted in my primary area of expertise, the history of chemistry.

The life of Tsuda Umeko, a pioneer in the field of English education for Japanese women, has been documented in a variety of media, including nonfiction, novels, and children's literature. There is a substantial corpus of scholarly literature on Umeko. A significant number of biographies have been published about her (Yoshikawa 1930, 1956, 1990; Yamazaki 1962; Oba 1990, 2021; Furuki 1991, 1992; Rose 1992; Kameda 2005; Takahashi 2022).[1] There are also numerous works focusing on the people around Umeko, as well as books that discuss her from the perspective of women's history (Iino, et al. (eds.) 2000; Kawamoto et al. 2001; Kameda 2005; Nimura 2015; Shirai 2018; Takahashi 2002). Umeko's studies of biology in the United States are also mentioned in various works, but

---

1 The authors of the books cited are all affiliated with Tsuda University (alumni, faculty, and staff). Of these, the 1930 biography by Yoshikawa (an administrative staff member at Umeko's Joshi Eigaku Juku) may be considered almost autobiography, as the author states, "The majority of the manuscript was reviewed by Ms. Tsuda before her death" (Preface). The biographies by Yoshikawa and Yamazaki are partially included in the official histories of the school (Tsuda Eigaku Juku (ed.) 1941; Tsuda Juku Daigaku (ed.) 1960).

few studies have focused on this issue or discussed it from the perspectives of the history of science or "science and gender."[2]

I published an article summarizing my findings on the relationship between Umeko and biology (Furukawa Yasu 2010), in which I endeavored to answer the questions set out above. The article prompted invitations to give lectures at several venues, including Tsuda University. However, the article and the lectures only attracted the attention of a small group of academics and concerned people. Thus, I decided to write a book to reach a broader audience. I have therefore attempted to write in an accessible style, expanding the narrative to include more social context, and incorporating the findings of subsequent research.

Fortunately, a significant amount of Umeko Tsuda's correspondence and personal documents have been meticulously preserved. Tsuda University has published two compilations of her writings, which are of significant value: *Tsuda Umeko bunsho* [The Writings of Tsuda Umeko] (Tsuda Juku Daigaku (ed.) 1980) and *The Attic Letters* (Tsuda Ume 1991). The former consists of Umeko's writings (mostly in English), talks, and related documents. The latter is a transcription of several hundred handwritten letters (in English) written by Umeko to her "American mother," which were discovered in 1984 in an old trunk in the attic of Tsuda University's main building on the Kodaira campus in the suburbs of Tokyo. The Tsuda University Archives also houses numerous additional unpublished manuscripts and internal documents. As previously indicated, her

2 One exception is Tsuda Juku Rika no rekishi wo kiroku suru kai (ed.) 1987, which devotes some pages (pp. 128–146) to the relationship between Tsuda Umeko and biology. Cf. Nakazawa 1988.

papers are also housed in the Special Collections at Bryn Mawr College. Additional materials on this topic can be found in various archives.

This book offers a different portrayal of Tsuda Umeko from those found in previous biographies. It adopts a historical framework – particularly the history of science – as its organizing structure, and it draws on primary sources while also re-examining the existing literature in depth to support its arguments. The objective of this study is to analyze the relationship between Umeko and science within the broader contexts of science, education, and society in Japan and the US at that time, and to consider the meaning of this relationship. In examining Umeko's life, it is essential to take into account the perspective of gender as well as the history of science. In this book, the term "gender" refers to socially and culturally constructed differences, rather than biological distinctions. This study does not seek to apply contemporary gender theories; rather, it identifies and examines historical gender issues relevant to science education and research.

The structure of the book is as follows. Chapter 1 examines the career of Umeko's father, Sen, whose life and work in agriculture significantly shaped his daughter's path. It also discusses Umeko's first study abroad in the United States as a young girl, her return to Japan, and her aspiration to pursue further studies abroad.

Chapter 2 provides an in-depth analysis of the educational philosophy and characteristics of Bryn Mawr College, with a particular focus on the biology education at Bryn Mawr in the context of the broader historical and cultural landscape of American biology. Additionally, it explores Umeko's educational experiences, comprehensively detailing the practical knowledge and skills she acquired at the college. It elucidates why a Japanese female English teacher at the Peeresses' School in the late 19th century majored in natural science, especially biology, in the United States.

Chapter 3 introduces Umeko's research as she embarks on her journey toward becoming a biologist and discusses conflicts that Umeko faced before returning to Japan and her subsequent attachment to and disengagement from the field of biology upon her return. It then examines why she did not or could not pursue a scientific career after returning to Japan and explores the place of science in Umeko's life.

Chapter 4 shifts focus to the educational milieu of Joshi Eigaku Juku, which was established and cultivated in a context in which women's higher education was seen as superfluous. The chapter traces Umeko's educational journey, her students' responses, the dynamics among them, their farewells, and the circumstances leading to Umeko's death.

Chapter 5 outlines the professional trajectory of Hoshino Ai, Umeko's successor, and examines how Umeko's legacy was perpetuated at Tsuda College and the historical context of science in higher education.

An epilogue examines Umeko's place in the history of women scientists in Japan and summarizes the book's argument.

I hope that this book will encourage readers to reflect on the life and times of Tsuda Umeko, an educator, and to take away something meaningful.

Chapter 1

A Young Japanese Girl in America

> Through a strange fortune, I was sent abroad for study while very young. On my return it was my wish to do what I could with my limited ability towards the education of our girls, to give to others what I had been enabled to learn. At the time of my return, the state of society was different from the present. There was little opportunity to work for the higher education of our women, and not much chance for the pupils to make practical use of such training even if received.
>
> – Tsuda Umeko,
> speaking at the opening of her school in 1900

Tsuda Umeko was born in Edo (the former name of Tokyo) on December 31, 1864. She was the second daughter of Tsuda Sen (1837–1908) and Hatsuko (1843–1909). Her father, Sen, had longed for a boy and was so disappointed when she was born that he did not want to name her even after the first seven days had passed. It was customary to hold a naming celebration called *Oshichiya* on the seventh night after a baby was born. Her mother named her Mume, which means "plum," after a bonsai plum tree that stood by her bedside. She later renamed herself Umeko ("ko" is a suffix used for female names). She was the second of twelve children (seven sisters and five brothers).[1]

1 Her siblings, from oldest to youngest, were Kotoko (born 1862), Umeko (1864), Motochika (1866), Jiro (1869), Kingo (1871), Gingo (1871), Fukiko

This chapter opens with the story of Sen, who shaped Umeko's life in many intricate ways. It then outlines the circumstances of young Umeko's journey to the United States, her personal development there, her independence as an English teacher upon her return, her dream to study abroad again, and how it came to be realized.

Tsuda Sen and Agriculture

Tsuda Sen was an agronomist and educator who actively adopted Western learning and ideas and had a strong anti-establishment spirit.[2] Born to a samurai in the Sakura domain of Shimousa Province (now Chiba Prefecture), Tsuda Sen (née Kojima) actively learned English from Dutch and English doctors at a young age. In 1862, he married Tsuda Hatsuko, the daughter of a low-ranking samurai of the Edo shogunate, thus becoming a son-in-law of the Tsuda family. In 1867, at the age of 29, he visited the United State as an interpreter for the shogunate to negotiate the purchase of warships, travelling with Ono Tomogoro (1817–1898, a bureaucrat and *wasan* mathematician), Fukuzawa Yukichi (1835–1901, an educator and philosopher), and others. During his six-month stay in the

---

(1873), Jun (1876), Mariko (1878), Yonako (1880), Kiyoko (1881), and Tomiko (1884). The eldest, Kotoko, was adopted by her maternal uncle. Kingo and Gingo were twin boys who passed away shortly after birth. The eldest son Motochika died at the age of 35, the third daughter Fukiko at 21, and the sixth daughter Kiyoko at 7. Sen had two other children born out of wedlock (Tsuda Michio 2012, pp. 14–16). See Figure 1.11 for a photograph of the Tsuda family.

2 For more on Tsuda Sen, see: Tsuda Noboru (ed.) 1958; Miyakoda 2000; Kim 2003; Takasaki 2008; and Tsuda Michio 2012. Umeko wrote an article on Sen's career in English: T. U. 1904.

US, he was influenced by the American people and culture to such an extent that it changed his outlook on life. He was particularly impressed by the abundance of agriculture and the spirit of equality among the classes. In San Francisco, Sen cut off his topknot, four years before the "*Dampatsu Rei*" decree (the Japanese government's order for samurai to remove their topknots in 1871) was issued. Umeko was then two years old.

When the shogunate collapsed, he left government service and took a job at a hotel for foreigners in the Tsukiji foreign settlement area. There, he tried his hand at growing Western vegetables and fruits to meet the tastes of the guests. Thereafter, he established a farm at his home in Azabu, Tokyo, where he cultivated asparagus, apples, strawberries, and other vegetables. When strawberries were ripe, Umeko visited the farm every day (Yoshikawa 1930, pp. 31–32, 1956, pp. 38–40).

In 1873, two years after Umeko went to the US, Sen went to Vienna, Austria, to attend the World Exposition and learn Western agricultural technology as a technical trainee. After returning to Japan, he wrote a book commonly called *Nogyo Sanji* [Three Processes in Agriculture] (1874) based on the horticultural lectures he heard by Daniel Hooibrenk, a Dutch agronomist then living in Vienna. Hooibrenk was a friend of Philipp Franz B. von Siebold (1846–1911), a German naturalist who had visited Nagasaki as a physician. Sen's book is more than just a translation of lectures; it provides an explanation of how Western farming methods could be connected to conventional Japanese farming methods. It also explains the importance of "experimentation" and "demonstration" in agriculture. In sum, the book demonstrates Sen's dedication to improving Japanese agriculture through the application of

Figure 1.1 Tsuda Sen at the 1873 Vienna World's Fair. Courtesy Tsuda University Archives.

Western knowledge (Tsuda Sen 1874; cf. Denda 1962, p. 63 ff; Saito 1968, pp. 66–76).

Tessa Morris-Suzuki, a scholar of modern Japanese history, refers to the process of transforming indigenous technology into technology based on modern Western science as "technology translation" (1995, p. 104). The technological knowledge of the Edo era (1603–1868) was reinterpreted in the Meiji era (1868–1912) in a form that was compatible with Western technology. Traditional technologies were reinterpreted through the paradigm of modern science. Sen's efforts to combine Western science with traditional Japanese farming methods can be seen as part of the "technology translation" movement.

The three processes of agriculture, as Sen explains in the *Nogyo Sanji*, are: (1) burying pipes in the ground to artificially promote the flow of air into the ground (culvert ventilation), (2) bending tree branches to improve sap flow,

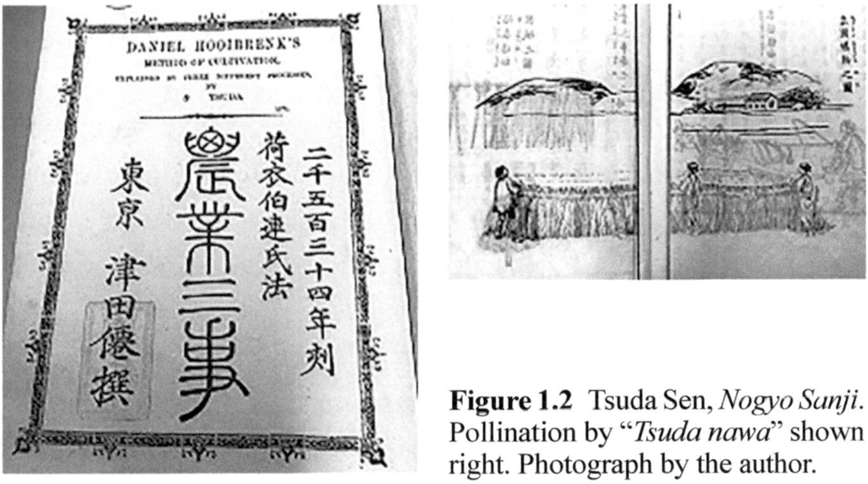

Figure 1.2 Tsuda Sen, *Nogyo Sanji*. Pollination by "*Tsuda nawa*" shown right. Photograph by the author.

and (3) artificially helping plants and trees to pollinate during flowering (pollination), thereby promoting crop yields. The artificial pollination was to be achieved with the "*Tsuda nawa* (Tsuda rope)," created by attaching tassels of wool yarn to the end of a rope, which was then coated with honey, to which pollen from rice and wheat plants was attached to ensure pollination (see Fig. 1.2).

At one time, about 200 female workers in a factory produced several thousand *Tsuda nawa* a day (Yoshikawa 1956, p. 126). Although the method was criticized by Gottfried Wagener (1831–1892), a hired foreign advisor, and others, sparking the so-called "pollination-aid method controversy," Sen defended his theory and founded both the Gakunosha Agricultural School and *Nogyo Zasshi* (Agricultural Journal) to promote it. Sen also joined the Meirokusha, an intellectual society led by Mori Arinori (1847–1889) and Fukuzawa Yukichi. There, he delivered speeches on his pollination method and published the transcripts of his lectures in the society's journal, *Meiroku Zasshi* (Tsuda Sen 1875).

Sen cited Charles Darwin (1809–1882) as theoretical evidence supporting his method:

> It is unfortunate that the method of rice flower mating, which was previously widely practiced throughout the country, has been hindered in its progress by officials who lack scientific knowledge. As a result, this practice has not been widely adopted. However, in his *Effect of Fertilization*, which was published a few years after *Nogyo Sanji*, Mr. Charles Darwin presents a highly detailed table concerning the effect of plant pollination. It furnishes evidence that the pollinated plants will become superior after several generations. Therefore, I am convinced that as scientific knowledge progresses, the dissemination of this pollination method will become increasingly widespread in the near future. (Tsuda Sen 1897, p. 35)[3]

The first edition of Darwin's *On the Origin of Species* was published in 1859. However, the book referred to here is *The Effects of Other Fertilization and Self-Fertilization in Plants*, published in 1876, in which Darwin argued that the results of his extensive crossbreeding experiments on plants showed that assisted fertilization produced more favorable individuals than self-fertilization. Since Darwin's argument about plant evolution is different from the mating aid method described by Sen (increasing production through pollination using *Tsuda nawa*), there is a leap in logic. Nevertheless, it is evident that Sen incorporated Darwin's most recent research findings in his own manner (cf. Saito 1968, p. 72).

---

3 Note that although this quotation comes from a report on the Vienna Exposition, it was published 24 years after the Exposition, and thus also comments on the situation in Japanese agriculture many years later.

The Ministry of Home Affairs' Industrial Promotion Bureau (Kangyo Ryo) began testing Sen's recommended artificial pollination method. They did not find *Tsuda nawa* to be effective and ended the test in 1879. Although the use of *Tsuda nawa* declined, the controversy about it raised awareness of Tsuda Sen and the Gakunosha Agricultural School and stimulated interest in scientific agricultural improvement as a result (Hara 1994; Saito 1968, pp. 66–76; Takasaki 2008, pp. 51–55).

Thereafter, Sen began developing an anti-bureaucratic and anti-authoritarian critique of agricultural policy in the *Nogyo Zasshi*, based on his Christian liberal philosophy (Kano 2018, p. 2). He developed a deep interest in Christianity early on and became a Christian in 1875 when he and his wife were baptized by an American Methodist pastor (Miyakoda 2000, pp. 39–50). Sen's activities to improve agriculture were part of the people's movement against the government. He believed that Protestantism supported this movement (Namimatsu 2013, pp. 95, 107ff). To Sen, Christianity and the agricultural improvement movement were inseparable.

Sen personally adhered to a Puritan way of life. Although he was a heavy drinker, he gave up alcohol after becoming a Christian and published *Hinomaru*, a magazine which campaigned for the prohibition of alcohol (Miyakoda 2000, pp. 151–169; Goto 2019). In his later years, he joined the campaign against the Ashio Copper Mine poisoning. He organized speeches at the Kanda Christian Youth Association to raise public awareness and worked hard in the movement to rescue farmers in affected areas (Miyakoda 2000, pp. 174–182).

In addition to the agricultural school, Sen devoted himself to several other educational projects, including the Girls'

Figure 1.3 Tsuda Sen (front row, third from right) at Gakunosha Agricultural School, which opened in Azabu, Tokyo in September 1875, where agricultural science and technology were taught, mainly in English; the school closed in December 1884 due to financial difficulties. Courtesy Tsuda Family Collection.

Elementary School, founded in 1874 and renamed the Kaigan Girls' School in 1878; the Special School (Tokushu Gakko), founded in 1875; and the Kokyo School, founded in 1878, renamed the Tokyo English School in 1881, which merged with the Bikai Seminary to become the Tokyo Eiwa School in 1883. He played a key role in founding and operating those private schools based on Christian principles. The Girls' Elementary School and the Tokyo Eiwa School, and Special School were the predecessors of the present-day Aoyama Gakuin and the University of Tsukuba School for the Blind, respectively (Kega 2014).

Umeko's way of life and thinking closely resembled those of her father, a Christian Enlightenment activist. Additionally, Sen's personal networks in Japan and abroad would play a significant role in Umeko's later life.

Japanese Girls in America

It was Sen who decided to send the young Umeko abroad to study. Kuroda Kiyotaka (1840–1900, later the second Prime Minister of Japan), then Vice Minister of Hokkaido *Kaitakushi* (Hokkaido Development Commission), had proposed the idea of sending young girls to the United States as government-sponsored students (Tsuda Juku Daigaku (ed.) 1984, pp. 82–83). When Kuroda had visited the US, he was surprised to find that American women were well educated and had high social status, which he attributed to their education. Kuroda emphasized the influence of mothers on preschool-age children, stressing the importance of educating girls and providing home education to raise wise mothers. Kuroda's views reflected the American view of the family in the Victorian era. Historian Takahashi Yuko has analyzed Kuroda's views on gender and found that he "converged with the Western image of a wise mother" and expected Japanese women to play the role of a mother who could nurture her sons for pioneering projects or for building a modern nation. Kuroda intended for women's roles to be integrated into state politics (Takahashi 2002, p. 26). This view of the wise mother was shared by many Meiji Enlightenment figures, including Kuroda's friend Mori Arinori, who was the Japanese commissioner to the United States and later Minister of Education.[4]

In the autumn of 1871, Kuroda's proposal was approved by the government, and recruitment of girls to be exchange students began. The period of study was 10 years, the destination was the United States, and the government would pay

---

4 For the Japanese ideal of "good wife, wise mother" (*ryosai kenbo*) and the nation in the Meiji era, see Koyama 2013.

all travel, tuition, and living expenses, as well as provide an annual scholarship of $800. They would travel with the Iwakura Mission (Iwakura Shisetsudan), which was scheduled to depart for the United States and Europe at the end of the year. According to the Meiji government's "Regulations for Studying Abroad (*kaigai ryugaku kisoku*)" (1870), the normal period of stay for government-financed study abroad was five years. Ten years of study abroad was an unprecedented and tremendously long period. Unlike the boys and young men who were dispatched to learn specific areas such as the legal system, economics, science, technology, and medicine necessary for modern nation-building, these girls were not tasked with the acquisition of specific studies or skills. Rather, the government wanted the girls to "acquire a taste of American family life" over a period of 10 years. In Takahashi's words, it was "to inject into Japanese women the ideology of 'domesticity' that was the norm for white middle-class women in the 19th century" (Takahashi 2002, p. 33).

There were few applications. Five applicants were selected: Ueda Teiko (16 years old at the time of departure, 1855–1939), Yoshimasu Ryoko (14 years old, 1857–1886), Yamakawa Sutematsu (11 years old, 1860–1919), Nagai Shigeko (10 years old, 1861–1937), and Tsuda Umeko (6 years old). These young girls were essentially forced to go to a foreign country with a different culture and race by their fathers and eldest brothers. The men who made these decisions were all from the old shogunate who had worked as low-ranking officials under the new government after the Meiji Restoration (1868). They wanted to regain their lost social status. Several of them had traveled to either Europe or the US, and even the others had considerable knowledge about foreign countries and recognized the value of a US education (Takahashi 2002, pp. 29–30).

For example, Yamakawa Sutematsu was the daughter of a feudal lord of Aizu. At the age of eight, she and her mother and older sisters had been besieged at Tsurugajo Castle during the Boshin War (a civil war in Japan between supporters of Tokugawa shogunate and troops of the anti-Tokugawa movement, 1868–1869). She was badly wounded. Her second older brother, Yamakawa Kenjiro (1854–1931), joined the *Byakkotai* (White Tiger Brigade, a military unit comprised of boys from Aizu samurai families), which fought against the anti-shogunate forces. He had been discharged because of his young age, just before the *Byakkotai* was annihilated. Kenjiro went to the US before Sutematsu as a student of the Hokkaido *Kaitakushi*. He studied at the Sheffield Scientific School of Yale College in New Haven, Connecticut. Later, he became the first Japanese professor of physics at the University of Tokyo and eventually became president of Tokyo Imperial University.[5] It was her eldest brother, Yamakawa Hiroshi (1845–1898, who would later become the principal of the Higher Normal School and a member of the House of Peers), who decided to send Sutematsu to the United States. Sutematsu's childhood name was Sakiko, but before she went to the US, her mother changed her name to Sutematsu. The name change was a tragic decision. Her mother thought that

---

5 Yamakawa Kenjiro left Japan for the US in January 1871 and returned in May 1875. He initially believed that Christianity was a pagan religion and opposed Sutematsu's study in the US on religious grounds. However, he changed his mind after discussing the matter with Mori Arinori who was stationed in the US (Takahashi 2002, pp. 82–84). On Yamakawa Kenjiro see Yamakawa 1937; Hanami (ed.) 1939; Watanabe Masao 1976a, 1990, Ch.1).

she would abandon (*sute*) this daughter but wait (*matsu*) for her (see Kuno 1993b, p.55).

As mentioned above, Tsuda Sen was also a former shogunate official who was fascinated by American culture and society. He also understood girls' education. As a commissioned officer of the Hokkaido Development Office, he was one of the first to hear about the scholarship opportunity and applied on behalf of his daughter. In fact, Sen wanted to send his eldest daughter, Kotoko, who was two years older than Umeko. But she furiously refused, so the role was given to his second daughter, Umeko. Although Umeko did not want to be away from her parents, it appears that she did not mind going (Takahashi 2002, pp. 28 and 231, n. 33).

Before their departure, the five girls had an audience with the Empress, and each was handed a letter of instructions (*osata-sho*). The letter read, "Your aim to study Western studies is really admirable. When you return to Japan, please be mindful that you will be an example for women, and study hard day and night" (Tsuda Juku Daigaku (ed.) 1984, p. 83). The main purpose of the letter was to encourage them to study hard so that they would serve as a role model for women upon their return to Japan. However, Umeko seems to have interpreted it to mean that she had been given a mission to educate Japanese women upon her return to Japan (Takahashi 2002, pp. 36–37). As will be discussed later, Umeko's sense that her study abroad was for the benefit of the Japanese nation would persist during her second period of study in the US.

The Iwakura Mission comprised 46 delegates and 18 attendants, along with 43 students, including the five girls. The mission was led by Iwakura Tomomi (1825–1883), ambassador extraordinary and plenipotentiary, and his deputy

Figure 1.4 Five female students, 1872. From left, Nagai Shigeko, Yoshimasu Ryoko, Ueda Teiko, Tsuda Umeko and Yamakawa Sutematsu. All wore kimonos when they left Japan but were photographed in Western clothes in Chicago. Courtesy Tsuda University Archives.

envoys, including Kido Takayoshi (1833–1877), Okubo Toshimichi (1830–1878), and Ito Hirobumi (1841–1909, later the first Prime Minister of Japan). The mission set sail from Yokohama on December 23, 1871 aboard the ship "America" of the Pacific Yusen Company. Umeko celebrated her seventh birthday on the Pacific Ocean. The delegation arrived in San Francisco on January 31, stayed in the US for about eight months, and then crossed the Atlantic to visit various European countries before returning in September 1873.

The students were separated from the delegation and travelled to their respective destinations. Of the five girls who stayed in the US, Teiko and Ryoko returned to Japan after less than a year due to health problems, largely caused by homesickness. Sutematsu, Shigeko, and Umeko were sent to different families, where they adjusted to life in America and grew up healthy. The three remained firm friends for the rest of their lives and played remarkable roles in Japanese women's history.

Umeko was placed in the care of Charles Lanman (1819–1895) of Georgetown, a suburb of Washington, DC. Lanman had been employed as a secretary for Mori Arinori at the Japanese legation.[6] The Lanmans, who had no children of their own, raised Umeko as if she were their own child. Thus, Umeko was raised in a white middle-class Protestant family in the Victorian era. In the fall of 1872, Umeko entered a small private elementary school called Stephenson Seminary (officially: Collegiate Institute), named after the principal Stephenson. The "Instructions for Western Travels (*Yoko Kokoroe-sho*)" which had been given to her before she left Japan, forbade conversion to Christianity, but at the age of eight, Umeko was voluntarily baptized (Yoshikawa 1956, pp. 91–95).[7] Sutematsu and Shigeko also joined the church, albeit somewhat later (Kuno 1993b, p. 81; Ikuta 2003, p. 54).

---

6 Mori Arinori at the Japanese legation played a pivotal role in the selection of American families to host the girls. See Kuniyoshi 2018, pp. 106–112.

7 The "Instructions for Western Travels" appears in Tsuda Juku Daigaku (ed.) 1984, pp. 84–85. In February 1873, the Meiji government repealed the prohibition of Christianity (*takafuda tekkyo* or removal of notice board), but opinions differ as to whether this had anything to do with Umeko's baptism. The commentary in Tsuda Juku Daigaku (ed.) 1984 (p. 560) states that there was no relationship. However, Terasaka Yumi claims that news of the repeal was reported to Mori Arinori, who conveyed it to Umeko. Terasaka goes on to say that Umeko, who wanted to assimilate into American culture, asked to join the church. The Lanmans consulted with Mori before having Umeko baptized on July 13 of that year at the Independent Church, which was not affiliated with any denomination (Terasaka 2001, p. 272ff).

In June 1878, Umeko graduated from Stephenson Seminary, and from September 1878, she attended Archer Institute, a private high school for girls. Umeko later wrote in her curriculum vitae that she took 17 courses at this school: English, literature, grammar, logic, French, Latin, astronomy, geography, physics, psychology, physiology, history, arithmetic, algebra, geometry, trigonometry, and natural history (Gakushuin Archives).[8] Of these, she was especially good in languages, mathematics, physics, and astronomy (Furuki 1992, p. 54).

Umeko grew up to be a bright, honest, and strong girl. Her "father," Charles Lanman, praised her as the "sunbeam" from the land of the rising sun that brightened their home. He wrote, "In the brilliancy of intellect and the rare integrity of her character, she was simply a wonderful child," and "with all her matured ideas, she was as frolicsome as a lamb and enjoyed all the amusements suited to her age" (Furuki 1991, p. 31). Although Umeko grew up with American values and ideas, she later noted that she was always aware that she was Oriental and Japanese, different from Americans "in race and blood" (Tsuda Ume 1991, pp. 81–82).

After graduating from high school, both Sutematsu and Shigeko attended Vassar College, a private women's college in Poughkeepsie, New York. Shigeko returned to Japan in October 1881 as scheduled, after completing a three-year arts program (majoring in music) (Ikuta 2003 and 2012, ch. 3; Kameda 2000, pp. 75–77). Sutematsu and Umeko were each granted permission to extend their studies for one year until

8 This resume, dated September 1885, was probably submitted when Umeko took a job at the Peeresses' School.

Figure 1.5 Umeko at age 7 when she was first placed with the Lanman family in Georgetown, near Washington, DC. Note she is wearing the same clothes as in Figure 1.4. Courtesy Tsuda University Archives.

Figure 1.6 Umeko at around age 11 in 1876. Courtesy Tsuda University Archives.

Figure 1.7 The three students reuniting at the World's Fair in Philadelphia in the summer of 1876. From left to right: Umeko (aged 11), Sutematsu (aged 16) and Shigeko (aged 15). The World's Fair in Philadelphia (10 May–10 November) was a grand celebration of the centenary of American independence, with 35 countries participating and nearly 10 million visitors. The Meiji Government's pavilion was a traditional Japanese house, in which it exhibited silk textiles and ceramics. Courtesy Tsuda University Archives.

Figure 1.8 Yamakawa Sutematsu around the time of her graduation from Vassar College, 1882. Courtesy Archives and Special Collections, Vassar College Library.

they graduated from their respective schools. Sutematsu attended Vassar College for four years, taking courses in French, German, Latin, English composition, English grammar, literary criticism, rhetoric, history, and philosophy, as well as a wide range of science courses, including mathematics, logic, physics, chemistry, botany, zoology, geology, and mineralogy.[9] Although the system at the time did not provide for a particular major, she liked biological subjects (Kuno 1993b, pp. 100, 108). In June 1882, she graduated with honors from a liberal arts program and became the first Japanese woman to receive a Bachelor of Arts degree from the United States. From July, she studied nursing at the New Haven Hospital

9 Transcript of Sutematz Yamakawa, A.B.1882, Registrar's Office, Vassar College. Sutematsu spelled her name in English as "Sutematz." At that time, Vassar College did not have a "major" system, and students were required to study a variety of subjects as part of their liberal arts education.

School of Nursing. By this time, she seemed to have developed confidence that she would be able to teach at least physiology at a women's normal school in Japan when she returned to Japan.[10]

Umeko graduated from the Archer Institute in June 1882. On October 31 of that year, she and Sutematsu left San Francisco on the Arabic for home. On November 21, Umeko was 17 years old and Sutematsu was 23 when they stepped onto Japanese soil for the first time in 11 years. Umeko, as the youngest of the three, was the only one to return to Japan without a university education.

An English Teacher at Peeresses' School

After returning to Japan with a strong sense of mission, Umeko hoped to become a teacher for the time being. However, the government was not prepared to accept Umeko and others. In contrast to the male students who were promptly appointed to some post upon their return to Japan, Umeko was disappointed with how she was treated. There was a sharp discrepancy between the government's intention that these students would return from America to become "wise mothers" and role models for Japanese women, and Umeko's understanding that she was tasked with the mission of educating Japanese women.

---

10 Letter from Sutematz Yamakawa to Alice Bacon, August 2, 1882, Oyama Collection, Archives and Special Collections, Vassar College Libraries. In this letter, in which she describes her dream after returning to Japan, she says that she could teach physical education as well as physiology.

Figure 1.9 Umeko aged around 18, ca. 1883. Courtesy Tsuda University Archives.

Another concern for Umeko was language. She was almost a native speaker of English, and was considered the best or second best English speaker of the Japanese people who had studied abroad and returned to Japan.[11] However, she had forgotten Japanese and could not read or write it. She thus had to learn Japanese and calligraphy from Shimoda Utako (1854–1936) at a private school for girls, and in exchange, taught English to Shimoda and the girls at the school. She reunited with Ito Hirobumi, with whom she become acquainted on the

11 Umeko's excellent English was mentioned, for example, in Sutematsu's letter to Alice Bacon, in which she says, "He [Kanda Naibu] speaks the best English of anyone I ever saw in Japan, perhaps excepting Ume." Sutematz to Alice Bacon, February 20, 1883, Oyama Collection, Archives and Special Collections, Vassar College Libraries. Kanda Naibu was an English scholar who later became a professor at the Tokyo Higher Commercial School (Kuno 1993b, p. 128).

Iwakura Mission. At his request, she lived at the Ito family's house to teach English to his wife (Ume, a former geisha) and daughter, as well as to interpret Mrs. Ito's conversations with foreigners. This was how she spent her days until she found official employment.

A month after Umeko returned to Japan, Nagai Shigeko married a lieutenant in the Navy, Uryu Sotokichi (1857–1937, later Admiral of the Navy), whom she had met while in the US. Shigeko later devoted herself to music education, focusing on the piano, at the Tokyo Academy of Music (Tokyo Ongaku Gakko), Tokyo Girls' High School, and Tokyo Women's Normal School (the predecessor of the Tokyo Women's Higher Normal School).

Sometime after her return to Japan, Sutematsu was approached by the Ministry of Education to see if she would be interested in teaching physiology and zoology at the Tokyo Women's Normal School, which had an opening for a teaching position. Her heart was shaken, yet she had no choice but to decline the offer because she was not confident in her Japanese reading and writing skills.[12] A year after her return to Japan, Sutematsu hesitated, but married Oyama Iwao (1842–1916), an army lord 18 years her senior. Sutematsu, who wore beautiful dresses and attended balls at the Rokumeikan (a Western-style government guesthouse with a ballroom, dining room, music room, and suites) who interacted with foreign diplomats, came to be known as "the Flower of the Rokumeikan" (Kuno 1993b, pp. 151–168). At the time, Umeko was unhappy with Sutematsu's way of life.

---

12 Sutematz to Alice Bacon, February 3, 1883, Oyama Collection, Archives and Special Collections, Vassar College Libraries.

However, Sutematsu, from her position as the wife of Count (later Duke) Oyama, supported women's education in Japan in various ways, including helping Umeko to get a job and start her English school.

Umeko did not choose to marry and have a family as the other two women did. In September 1885, in accordance with the Ministry of Education's policy of separate education for boys and girls, the girls' division of the Gakushuin (a school for the nobility's children) became an independent school, Peeresses' School (Kazoku Jogakko). Three years after returning to Japan, at the age of 20, Umeko was finally hired as an English teacher at this school. Her hiring was probably due to the efforts of Ito, Shimoda Utako (who later became the school's academic supervisor and professor), and Oyama Sutematsu, a member of the founding preparatory committee. Umeko was initially hired as an assistant professor, but in November of the same year, she was promoted to professor and was paid an annual salary of 420 yen. The school was divided into two departments, elementary (six years) and junior high (six years). English was taught in the junior high department (Joshi Gakushuin (ed.) 1935, p. 219).[13]

The school was for the daughters of the nobility (*kazoku,* the hereditary peerage including former feudal lords and court nobles) and at the time was a government school under the jurisdiction of the Ministry of the Imperial Household. Although in principle, the school accepted girls from the nobility, in its first year of operation, it also accepted other students. As a

---

13 For more on the Peeresses' School, see Gakushuin hyaku nenshi hensan iinkai (ed.) 1981, Ch. 4; Gakushuin Joshi Chuto-ka and Koto-ka (ed.) 1985; and Takahashi 2013.

result, about 60 students from the Toyo Girls' School (Toyo Jojuku), a private school run by Shimoda Utako were enrolled. Article 2 of the school's student handbook reads:

> Those who study at this school are to be good wives to their husbands, wise mothers to their children, filial piety to their parents, and gentle and compassionate kinswomen to their servants. To embody the virtues of nobility, it is essential to avoid being misled by fantasy and illusions, and to adhere to realistic practices. (Joshi Gakushuin (ed.) 1935, p. 221)

Thus, the school's aim was to educate students to have the virtues of *ryosai kenbo* (a good wife, wise mother), a dominant gender norm for Japanese women before World War II.

Umeko's daily life at the Peeresses' School in Nagata-cho, Tokyo, was quite full. While teaching there, however, she began to experience frustration and dissatisfaction with her young students. They exhibited obedient and ladylike qualities, akin to dolls, yet they demonstrated a lack of initiative and limited intellectual activity (cf. Kuroiwa 2008; Kazoku shiryo kenkyukai (ed.) 2011). At the same time, she was surprised and saddened to see Japan's male-centered society and the low social status of women, something she had felt since soon after returning to Japan, and to learn that Japanese women themselves were so unaware of this as a problem. Umeko, who had spent most of her childhood in the US, experienced a great reverse culture shock (see Shimizu 2001; Serizawa and Toda 2002).

Figure 1.10 The opening ceremony at the Peeresses' School on November 13, 1885 ("Kazoku Jogakko Gyokei"). Empress Shoken is standing before the table on the stage. Courtesy Imperial Household Archives. Umeko wrote a letter to Mrs. Lanman detailing the day, concluding that she was "very tired after everything." (Tsuda Ume 1991, pp. 230–231).

Figure 1.11 Tsuda Umeko and her family. At the site where the Gakunosha Agricultural School was located, September 1886, one year after Umeko joined the teaching staff of the Peeresses' School. Front row, from left: Umeko, Kotoko (elder sister), Hatsuko (mother), Sen's sister, Tomiko (younger sister), Kiyoko (younger sister), Yonako (younger sister), Mariko (younger sister). Back row, from left, Motochika (brother), Jiro, (brother), Ueno Eizaburo (Kotoko's husband), Sen (father), Jun (brother), Fukiko (younger sister). Courtesy Tsuda Family Collection.

Realizing the Dream of Studying in America Again

Umeko's personality was straightforward but passionate, and she was extremely strong-willed. Soon after she started teaching, she decided that teaching would be her career for the rest of her life, and she seems to have been determined to remain single. She resisted the idea that Japanese women were supposed to marry, obey their husbands, bear and raise children, and protect their homes, which was considered a virtue. Although courted by scholars who had studied abroad, she did not change her mind.[14] Her father, Sen, was devoted to Western culture and thought, yet he had no doubts about the Japanese patriarchal and marital system. Nonetheless, he did not interfere in any way with Umeko's decisions about marriage.

While teaching, Umeko became aware of her disadvantage in not having a college education, and began to dream of returning to the US to study. She must have also been filled with longing for the America where she spent her childhood. In her letters to Adeline Dodge Lanman (1824–1914), her American "mother," she began to frankly express her feelings about her desire to study in America again.

---

14 The suitors appear to have included Kanda Naibu (1857–1923) and Nakajima Rikizo (1858–1918). Kanda, an English scholar, graduated from Amherst College and served as a professor at Imperial University College of Letters, Tokyo Higher Normal School, and Gakushuin. Nakajima, an ethicist, studied at Yale College at his own expense and later became a professor at Tokyo Imperial University. Aiya Sakae, Umeko's niece, wrote: "According to Ms. Tsujimura, who remembers the time well, she was small, with full cheeks and a pretty mouth. She must have been a lovely person. She was also the only woman of her time who had studied abroad, so it is not surprising that she attracted the attention of many distinguished gentlemen who had returned to Japan from abroad" (Aiya 1929, p. 139).

Figure 1.12 Adeline Dodge Lanman, Umeko's foster mother in the USA. Courtesy Tsuda University Archives.

In the spring and summer of 1888, Umeko began to make moves toward realizing this dream. She was eager to receive two or more years of college education at one of the best American institutions in order to become a "first-rate teacher" (Tsuda Ume 1991, pp. 248–250).[15] That she did not have a specific college in mind at the outset is evident from her request that Mrs. Lanman obtain admissions information from Smith College, Wellesley College, Mount Holyoke College, and the appropriate normal school (Tsuda Ume 1991, pp. 314–316). In a letter to Mrs. Lanman dated July 10, 1888, Umeko wrote:

15 Letter from Umeko to Adeline Lanman, dated May 6, 1888. In *The Attic Letters* (Tuda Ume 1991, pp. 248–250), the date of this letter is erroneously listed as 1886.

> As to coming to America for study, I hope you will think about [this]. I think if I came again, I should enter some institution in the North for special branches, [such] as a normal school, to make the science of teaching a specialty and see how it is done in some of the large schools. … I want to come, I want to study some more and fit myself better to be a teacher, not for pleasure. (Tsuda Ume 1991, p. 314)

At the same time, Umeko mentioned that the issue of funding for study abroad was an obstacle and that she was concerned about whether those who had been given the opportunity to study abroad once by the government would be allowed to do so a second time.

Alice Mabel Bacon (1858–1918) was a colleague of Umeko's in Japan and provided necessary support. Bacon was the daughter of Sutematsu's former American host family, and had gone to Japan as an English teacher at the Peeresses' School through Sutematsu's arrangement. Alice was also later involved in the establishment of Umeko's English school (see Takahashi 2002, ch. 5; Bacon 1891, 1893). She encouraged Umeko to study in the US again. Yoshikawa writes the following about Umeko's state of mind at that time:

> It has been three years since I started teaching. What have I done during that time? I do not consider myself to have been unenthusiastic in my duties, but I am an English teacher in both name and reality. Teaching English is not a bad thing. However, I am not satisfied with the amount of English knowledge I can impart. In fact, while I teach English enthusiastically every day, I feel a sense of loneliness in the back of my mind. I wonder why the pioneer mission sent me

> to study abroad for so long. In her letter to me, the Empress wrote, "After your return to Japan, you will serve as a role model for women." In light of this, I cannot be satisfied with being a mere English teacher. There must be more work that I can devote my soul to. … What is it that I should do? I want to break out of my current life and open up new circumstances. To do so, I would like to do some specialized research. There are no women in Japan today who are scholars. I do not know whether I have such qualities or not, whether I am capable of bold research or not, or whether it is my mission to become a scholar or not. However, I would like to more or less develop my innate talents. I should not be prohibited from studying because I am a woman. I have no desire to be a scholar. However, I would like to have the opportunity of education and fully develop my talents. That is my present desire. Only by developing my talents will I be able to make a new life for myself. I will be able to see my future. I will find a job that I can put my heart and soul into. (Yoshikawa 1956, pp. 172–173)

Meanwhile, Clara A. N. Whitney (1860–1936) conveyed Umeko's wishes to Mrs. Mary Harris Morris (1836–1924), an influential Quaker woman who had known Umeko since her initial stay in the United States. Clara was the daughter of William Cogswell Whitney (1825–1882), whom Sen had invited to teach English at the Gakunosha Agricultural School.[16] Incidentally, she came to Japan with her father and married Kaji Umetaro (1864–1925), the third son of the navy

---

16 For more on the events leading up to this, see Kameda 2005, pp. 116–122; 2006, part 1, chapter 1.

minister Katsu Kaishu (1823–1899), in 1886.[17] Sen was a close friend of Clara's and translated her Western cookbook into Japanese (Whitney 1885). Umeko appears to have divulged her feelings to Clara at some point (Tsuda Ume 1991, p. 318). Clara was a close friend of Mrs. Morris, who lived in Overbrook, a suburb of Philadelphia. Upon receiving news from Clara, Mrs. Morris consulted with the president of Bryn Mawr College, a Quaker women's college near her home, about accepting Umeko. On June 30, 1889, the college agreed to allow Umeko to enroll with a waiver of tuition, dormitory fees, and meals (Kameda 2005, p. 122; 2006, p. 15). Thus, her dream of returning to the US to study again came to fruition. Once again, Sutematsu's and Sen's personal connections were involved.

I confirmed the whereabouts of two of Umeko's "study abroad" applications that have not been mentioned in previous studies. One is in the Gakushuin Archives, and the other is in the Imperial Household Agency's Archives. The former is titled "Application for Resignation (*jishoku negai-sho*)" and was submitted by Umeko to Nishimura Shigeki (1888–1902), the principal of Peeresses' School, on April 30, 1889 (Figure 1.13). However, the word "Resignation" in the title "Application for Resignation" was crossed out in red and the title was changed to "Application Form (*negai-sho*)." Additionally, the phrase "request for resignation" was changed to "request for study abroad while serving in the school." Therefore, it appears that she had decided to resign from the school to pursue her study abroad. However, the school granted her permission to pursue

17 Clara had six children with Umetaro, but later divorced him and returned to the United States with her children. See Whitney 1996; Sano 2019.

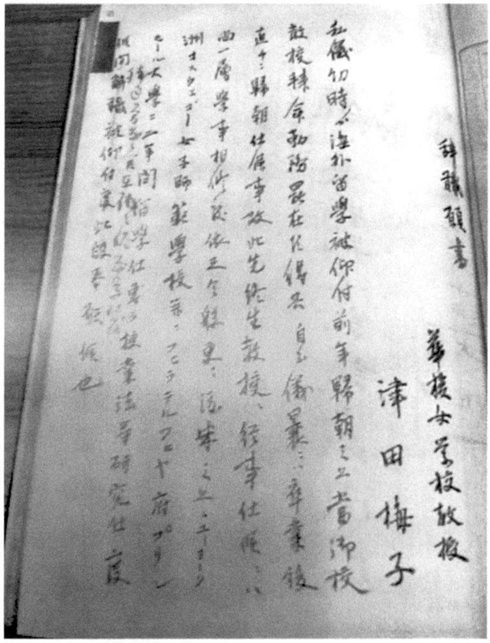

Figure 1.13 Umeko's "Application for Resignation," April 30, 1889. Courtesy Gakushuin Archives.

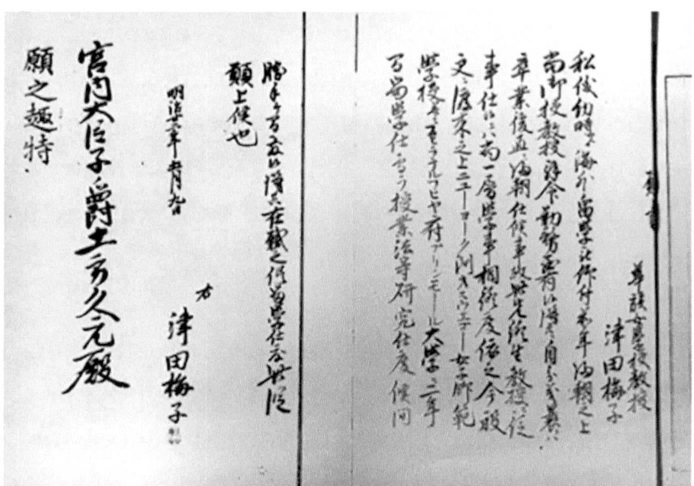

Figure 1.14 Umeko's official application to study abroad, May 9, 1889. Courtesy Imperial Household Archives.

her studies in America on the condition that she would receive a salary and resume her position upon her return to Japan. This arrangement was made by Otori Keisuke (1833–1911), the president of Gakushuin, in collaboration with Nishimura (Gakushuin Archives). Furthermore, the address was altered in red from "To Nishimura Shigeki, Principal of Peeresses' School" to "To Hijikata Hisamoto [1833–1918], Minister of the Imperial Household" and the date was changed from "April 30" to "May 9." This suggests that the application was drafted for Hijikata.

The official "application" (dated May 9, 1889) addressed to the Minister of the Imperial Household is in the collection of the Imperial Household Archives (Figure 1.14). The text is similar to the one in the Gakushuin Archives and reads:

> I was ordered to study abroad as a child, and after returning to Japan, I was appointed as a professor at the Peeresses' School. ... I am determined to continue serving as a professor and will do so by pursuing further studies. Therefore, I would like to go to the US to study more at the Oswego Women's Normal School in New York State and at the Bryn Mawr College in Philadelphia, where I will spend two years exclusively studying teaching methods, etc.

It should be noted that the purpose of studying abroad was clearly stated here as "exclusively studying teaching methods, etc." and that Oswego Normal School for Women is mentioned before Bryn Mawr College as the destination of study. Umeko would have been aware that the latter did not have an independent program specializing in pedagogy or teaching methods.

The Oswego Normal School in New York (officially called Oswego State Normal and Training School at the time) was a state school established in the 1860s to train elementary school teachers. It is known for its practical education based on the ideas of Swiss educator Johann Heinrich Pestalozzi (1746–1827). Takamine Hideo (1854–1910), the principal of Tokyo Higher Normal School, had visited to inspect it in 1875. It is likely that Takamine had informed Umeko of this school.[18]

Thus, Umeko's cherished dream of returning to America to study once more finally came true. However, Umeko's main destination was not Oswego, but Bryn Mawr, where she would study biology, not teaching methods in English. The next chapter will describe what awaited Umeko at Bryn Mawr College and her experiences on her second visit to America.

18 For more information on Takamine's visit to Oswego Normal School, see Takamine 1921, chapter 4. Mrs. Takamine was a member of the English Drama Club with Umeko (Kuno 1993b, p. 125). On Oswego Normal School, see Hollis 1898.

Chapter 2

Bryn Mawr College and Biology

> I feel that now my mind is more developed than at the time I came back, and that I would appreciate study more.
>
> – Tsuda Umeko,
>
> letter to Mrs. Lanman, May 6, 1888.

> I also enjoyed reading Darwin's biography. This was only after I developed an interest in science. I found it interesting that even Darwin struggled with memorizing the German language.
>
> – Tsuda Umeko,
>
> "The Biographies I Was Absorbed in Reading," 1908.

Tsuda Umeko's childhood study abroad was not of her own volition; she had been dispatched to the US by the government and her father. She grew up in an environment where everything was provided and prepared for her by adults. However, her second study abroad experience was different. Although it was, once again, a government-funded study abroad program with a full salary, this time she won it through her own initiative. She was able to experience the US again, but this time as a mature adult. This experience would prove more significant for her later career. In this chapter, we examine what Umeko encountered at Bryn Mawr College and how it shaped her.

Department of Biology at Bryn Mawr College

Umeko travelled to the United States in July 1889 and enrolled at Bryn Mawr College for the fall semester. She was then 24 years old. Umeko's status at the college was "special student." According to Bryn Mawr regulations, a special student is a student who is not pursuing a bachelor's degree. However, special students could transfer to the regular undergraduate program if they earned the necessary credits. Bryn Mawr had an entrance examination, but Umeko was exempt.[1]

She did not decide to major in biology until after commencing at the college. In fact, the word "biology" does not appear in the series of letters she wrote to Mrs. Lanman before arriving in the United States. Yoshikawa explains:

> At that time, Bryn Mawr had several departments, including literature, biology, Greek, and Latin. By the time Umeko left Yokohama, she was still unsure of her major, but after much consideration, she chose biology as her major and decided to take two or three other courses. (1956, pp. 174–175)

Her rationale for majoring in biology will be examined in the next section. This section will focus on Bryn Mawr College and its educational philosophy. By the 1880s, seven private women's colleges, the so-called "Seven Sisters," had been founded in the eastern United States. In chronological order, they were Mount Holyoke Seminary (founded in 1837, renamed Mount Holyoke College in 1888), Vassar College (founded in 1865), Wellesley College (founded in 1875), Smith College (founded in 1875), Radcliffe College (spun

---

1 For a definition of "special student," see Bryn Mawr College, 1890a, p. 16.

Figure 2.1 Aerial view of Bryn Mawr College campus, ca. 1890s. Courtesy Bryn Mawr College Special Collections.

off from Harvard in 1879), Bryn Mawr (founded in 1885), and Barnard College (spun off from Columbia in 1889). As mentioned in the previous chapter, Sutematsu and Shigeko studied at Vassar. In the United States, women who completed higher education in the 1870s and 1880s are referred to as the "first generation of women in higher education" (Sakamoto 2000, p. 28). Although they were not Americans, Sutematsu and Shigeko can be included in this group.

Bryn Mawr College, one of the Seven Sisters, was established in the Philadelphia suburb of Bryn Mawr in the fall of 1885 with an initial enrollment of 44 students, made possible by a generous bequest from the late Quaker physician Joseph W. Taylor (1810–1880). Umeko enrolled in the school only four years after its founding.

The school's philosophy differed from the other women's colleges, strongly reflecting the philosophy of Martha Carey Thomas (1857–1935), a professor of English who was then dean of the college and would become its second president in

1894. She is known as an early feminist who fought for women to receive the same education as men, based on her personal experiences of gender discrimination as a student. She was one of the activists of the so-called “first-wave feminism,” a movement for women’s social rights in Europe and the United States. Her parents, devout Quakers, were active in prohibition and religious activities. Despite their influences, Thomas rejected the Victorian view of the family, the idea of the home as the domain of women (Horowitz 1999, ch. 6).

Although Bryn Mawr was a women’s college, it did not aim to nurture what the Japanese called “good wives and wise mothers.” At the time, there was a movement among women in the US for home economics or “domestic science” as a discipline to scientize and improve housework.[2] Thomas not only rejected domestic science, which was associated with “femininity,” but also eliminated anything related to “domesticity.” To free students from domestic labor, they were not required to make their beds or engage in cooking, even in dormitory life because she aspired to make Bryn Mawr College an institution that rigorously educated academics at the highest level, training teachers and researchers equivalent to their male counterparts. She was convinced that biological research had proven that there were no differences between men and women in academic ability and intelligence.[3] She carefully selected her students according to standards of admission as rigorous as those of Harvard University and

---

2 For the American home economic movement of the late 19th and early 20th centuries, see, e.g., Shapiro 2009; Imai (ed.) 1992; and Takemata 1990.

3 This idea was expressed in a speech Thomas gave at Joshi Eigaku Juku when she visited Japan in 1915 (Tsuda University Archives).

Figure 2.2 Martha Carey Thomas. Photographed in 1889 while Umeko was at Bryn Mawr College. Courtesy Bryn Mawr College Special Collections.

modeled the curriculum on Johns Hopkins University, which had adopted the philosophy of German research universities, emphasizing graduate education, especially for researchers pursuing doctoral degrees. Johns Hopkins University was a private university founded in 1876 on the estate of Johns Hopkins (1795–1873), a Quaker businessman from Baltimore (Furukawa Yasu 2018, pp. 216–218). Thomas' father was a trustee of Johns Hopkins University. Bryn Mawr's founder, Taylor, was a Quaker of the same lineage as Hopkins, and many of Bryn Mawr's teachers were alumni of Johns Hopkins University. Bryn Mawr College thus acquired the nickname "Jane Hopkins."[4]

4 For the early history of Bryn Mawr College, see Meigs 1956; Takahashi 2002, ch. 6. On the sobriquet "Jane Hopkins," see Kohler 1990, p. 649.

Bryn Mawr College was a small institution, comprising a single college with seven language departments (English, Greek, Latin, German, French, Spanish, and Italian), three humanities and social science departments (history and political economy, philosophy, and history of religion), and four science departments (mathematics, biology, chemistry, and physics). It is important to recognize that at the time there were people in America who maintained that higher education would undermine women's health (Takahashi 2002, pp. 56). Few women pursued careers in science. In this context, Bryn Mawr's emphasis on natural sciences was pioneering in the United States. Vassar College, where Sutematsu and Shigeko studied, was basically a liberal arts college, but Bryn Mawr went further, emphasizing graduate education and training highly specialized researchers. Umeko, perhaps unknowingly, had jumped into the middle of this unique educational environment.

Indeed, Bryn Mawr's biology department held a notable position among the nation's universities. In fact, biology emerged as a scientific discipline in the United States, both academically and institutionally, between 1875 and 1895, concurrent with the genesis of Bryn Mawr College (Pauly 1984; 1987, p. 56). Biology education had until then been incidental to medical school education, but during this period independent and specialized biology departments were established in universities. Johns Hopkins University was a leader in the field, and had significant influence on universities throughout the United States. William Keith Brooks (1848–1908) and the English-born physiologist Henry Newell Martin (1848–1893) taught there, and the biologists they educated played an important role in the discipline's dissemination.

The Johns Hopkins-educated researchers Edmund Beecher Wilson (1856–1939), Thomas Hunt Morgan (1866–1945), Ross Granville Harrison (1870–1959), and Edwin Grant Conklin (1863–1952) initiated a new wave of experimental zoology, especially experimental embryology (Maienschein, 1991; Rainger et al. (eds.), 1988; Oppenheimer 1967; Mizoguchi 1981). Importantly, the theory of evolution had not yet become central to biology at the time.

Experimental embryology originated in the "developmental mechanics" (in German: *Entwicklungmechanik*) of the German zoologist Wilhelm Roux (1850–1924). Biology was traditionally regarded as a "study of observation," which had been content to observe and describe nature as it is. This new trend began to artificially subject organisms to "abnormal conditions" that did not exist in their natural state, and then analyze the changes. In other words, the approach changed from passive to active. For example, researchers examined the changes that occurred when egg cells were broken by applying a needle or other artificial means in the early stages of development and observed the developmental mechanism from there. This paradigm of German origin was adopted and developed by a generation of American biologists. Individuals who received training in this area of research, particularly at Johns Hopkins, subsequently dispersed to prominent universities throughout the United States, thereby contributing to advancing biological research.

The biology department at Bryn Mawr College was founded by such researchers. It was the first independent biology department in a women's college, and one of the few in the nation when the college was founded in 1885. Other universities with outstanding biology programs established their

Figure 2.3 Edmund Beecher Wilson, ca. 1890. Courtesy Bryn Mawr College Special Collections.

departments later: e.g., Clark University in 1889, Columbia University in 1891, and the University of Chicago in 1892.

The first two faculty members in the biology department at Bryn Mawr were Professor Edmund Wilson and Associate Lecturer Frederick Schiller Lee (1859–1939), both of whom received their doctorates from Johns Hopkins University. At Bryn Mawr, they developed the first biology curriculum for undergraduate students. Although biology at Bryn Mawr had originally been conceived by James Evans Rhodes (1828–1895), its first president (1884–1894), as a preparatory course in physiology and health to prepare students for medical school, Wilson developed it into an independent general biology program (Pauly 1984, p. 382; 1987, pp. 56–58, 61–62).

If they wanted to, Bryn Mawr's biology students could transfer to affiliated institutions such as the Woman's Medical College of Pennsylvania to continue their studies in medicine

Figure 2.4 Taylor Hall, 1890s. The first large building on campus, named after the founder, Joseph Taylor. Three stories of stone, topped by a clock tower. The Biology Department was located here. Courtesy Bryn Mawr College Special Collections.

Figure 2.5 Biology Laboratory (Taylor Hall, 3rd floor), 1886. The men standing at the back are Professor Wilson (left) and Lecturer Lee. Courtesy Bryn Mawr College Special Collections.

(Bryn Mawr College 1890a, p. 28). Incidentally, Okami (née Nishida) Keiko (1859–1941), one of the first Japanese female medical students, had studied at the Pennsylvania Women's Medical College in 1885. Five years older than Umeko, Okami was the first Japanese woman to receive an M.D. degree in March 1889, returning to Japan at the same time Umeko

Figure 2.6 Biology Laboratory (Taylor Hall, 3rd floor), ca. 1890. Courtesy Bryn Mawr College Special Collections.

Figure 2.7 Library (Taylor Hall, 1st floor), ca. 1890. Courtesy Bryn Mawr College Special Collections.

entered Bryn Mawr College. She, too, had corresponded with Mrs. Morris.[5]

Wilson was a student of Brooks and considered a leading authority on cytology. He had published the first American biology textbook, *General Biology* (1866), co-authored with

5 Pennsylvania Women's Medical College was one of the predecessors of the current Drexel University School of Medicine. After returning to Japan, Okami Keiko worked at Jikei Hospital in Tokyo and then served as vice principal of Shoei Girls' School (Shoei Joshi Gakuin) (Nagatoya 1958; Hotta 2016).

Table 2.1 Biology Faculty of Bryn Mawr College

Fall 1889 – Summer 1891
Edmund B. Wilson (Johns Hopkins University, Ph.D., 1881) Professor (Biology)
Frederick S. Lee (Johns Hopkins University, Ph.D., 1885) Associate (Physiology and Histology)
Leah Goff (Bryn Mawr College, A.B., 1889) Laboratory Demonstrator
Fall 1891 – Spring 1892
Thomas H. Morgan (Johns Hopkins University, Ph.D., 1890) Associate Professor (Biology)
Joseph W. Warren (University of Bonn, M.D., 1880) Associate Professor (Physiology)
Jacques Loeb (University of Strasbourg, M.D., 1884) Associate (Physiology and Physiological Psychology)
Ida A. Keller (University of Zurich, Ph.D., 1890) Non-resident Lecturer (Botany)

Note: In brackets after names: university of graduation, degree, year of degree. Parentheses after positions are the name of the discipline attached to the position. Compiled from Bryn Mawr College, *Bryn Mawr College Program*, 1890, 1891, 1892.

William Thompson Sedgwick (1855–1921) of Johns Hopkins University (see Muller 1943; Morgan 1940; Allen 1970). Wilson and Lee moved to Columbia University in 1891 when its biology department was founded, and President Rose and Dean Thomas took the opportunity to rebuild the biology faculty at Bryn Mawr, appointing Morgan, Joseph W. Warren (1849–1916), and Jacques Loeb (1859–1924) to the department. Morgan would later be awarded a Nobel Prize in physiology or medicine. Loeb, born in Germany, was later a professor at the University of Chicago and the University of California, Berkeley, and became a major figure in physiology in the United States (Pauly 1987). Thus, Umeko studied at Bryn Mawr under up-and-coming young biologists who would become leaders in the field (see Table 2.1).

Umeko at Bryn Mawr

The *Bryn Mawr College Program* (the equivalent of today's combined student handbook and course syllabus), published annually at the time, lists the students and their majors for each year. Umeko's major is listed as "English and History" for the first two years (1890a and 1891a) and "Biology" for the third year (1892a). It seems likely, however, that Umeko's decision to major in biology was made relatively soon after commencing at Bryn Mawr College.

We reach this conclusion through analysis of the structure of course enrollment at that time. The undergraduate program at Bryn Mawr College comprised three groups of courses: minor, major, and post-major courses, following the system at Johns Hopkins University. Here, minor, major, and post-major were terms for first-year, second-year, and third-year course groups, respectively (but not necessarily for academic year). In the Biology Department, students in the minor were required to take five hours of lectures in general biology plus six hours of laboratory work per week. All biology majors had to take these general courses first. The major was the next level of courses, consisting of specialized courses (and laboratory work) in zoology, morphology, comparative anatomy, physiology, histology, etc. Post-majors involved special studies. Undergraduate students were required to take minor and major courses in two different fields (e.g., biology and chemistry, biology and physics, biology and history) during their four years, and then enter a post-major in one field (e.g., biology). Additionally, students were required to take so-called general education courses such as English, philosophy, and history (Bryn Mawr College 1890a, pp. 15, 25–29).

Table 2.2 lists the biology courses Umeko took. As we can see, Umeko followed the biology department's program from the beginning. In the fall semester of her first year, she took "General Biology A" (Wilson), "General Biology B" (Lee), and "Laboratory Work" (Wilson and Lee). The following spring semester, she took the same three courses again. She was enrolled in these "minor" curricula for a year. During her first year, she also took other science courses, including "Inorganic Chemistry" (Edward H. Keiser) and "Chemistry Laboratory Work" (Keiser). Additionally, she took several liberal arts courses, but only "Ancient History" was a regular credit course; she attended the others as an auditor. In the fall of her second year, she began taking "major" courses, such as "General Zoology" (Wilson), "Comparative Anatomy of Vertebrates" (Lee), and "Laboratory Work" (Wilson and Lee). This suggests that, although she had initially registered – somewhat tentatively – as an English and History major, she was in fact taking the courses required for a major in biology.

Despite the absence of a document that directly evidences Umeko's rationale for selecting biology, the following factors, considered in the broader context, may explain her decision. First, as Yoshikawa stated, Umeko was not content with her career as an English teacher and aspired to ascertain her aptitude through academic endeavors. As we can see, she focused on aptitude for the natural sciences. According to those around her, Umeko was skilled in analysis and superior in reasoning. Mathematics and science had been her strongest subjects when she was a student at the Archer Institute. One possible explanation for her focus on biology, among the natural sciences, might be the influence of her father, Tsuda Sen, an agronomist whose work was closely related to biology.

Table 2.2 Courses Tsuda Umeko took (1889–1892)

Fall Semester (Oct. 1, 1889~Jan. 31, 1890)
General Biology A (Wilson) minor course General Biology B (Lee) minor course Laboratory Work (Wilson & Lee) minor course
Spring Semester (Feb. 17~May 23, 1890)
General Biology A (Wilson) minor course General Biology B (Lee) minor course Laboratory Work (Wilson & Lee) minor course
Fall Semester (Sept. 30, 1890~Jan. 30, 1891)
General Zoology (Wilson) major course Comparative Anatomy of Vertebrata (Lee) major course Laboratory Work (Wilson & Lee) major course
Spring Semester: Leave of Absence
Fall Semester (Sept. 20, 1891~Jan. 29, 1892)
General Biology A (Morgan) minor course, audited Advanced Physiology and Histology (Warren) major course, audited Laboratory Work (Morgan, Warren & Hyde) major course Post Major Biology (Loeb) post major course Post Major Biology (Morgan) post major course
Spring Semester (Feb. 15~May 30, 1892)
Physiology of the Central Nerve System (Loeb) graduate course Post Major Biology (Morgan) post major course Laboratory Work (Morgan) post major course
Other Courses Umeko took and earned credits for:
Chemistry Laboratory Work (Keiser), Ancient History, Modern History, English Literature, Essay, Philosophy, Psychology, Biblical Literature, and Politics
Other Courses Umeko audited (without taking examination):
Inorganic Chemistry (Keiser), Christian Ethics, Logic, Biblical Study, and Physical Training

Note: Names in brackets are those of the lecturers.
Compiled from Umé Tsuda, Transcript, 1889–1892, Bryn Mawr College Special Collections; Bryn Mawr College Record of Ume Tsuda, Tsuda University Archives; and Bryn Mawr College 1890a, 1891a, 1892a.

Figure 2.8 Umeko in a gown, 1889. The photograph was probably taken shortly after her admission to Bryn Mawr College. Taken by a photographer (Geo. Prince) in Washington DC. It was Dean Thomas' policy that Bryn Mawr students wear gowns during class. Courtesy Tsuda University Archives.

In addition, Umeko had heard directly from Sutematsu that the latter liked biology-related subjects at Vassar College, which may have influenced her decision. Moreover, as previously stated, the biology department at Bryn Mawr College was developing in the context of the rise of biology in the United States. Perhaps she became aware of this after enrolling at Bryn Mawr. It is highly plausible that Dean Thomas, her academic advisor, recommended and encouraged Umeko to pursue studies in the biology department. The more biology courses Umeko enrolled in, the more fascinated she became by the biological sciences.

What is clear is that Umeko decided to major in biology early in her first semester, deviating from her original purpose. This decision is remarkable in the context of the following

Figure 2.9 Umeko (right) reading with a cup of tea in the dormitory room of schoolmate Anna Powers, 1890. This dormitory was in Merrion Hall. Courtesy Bryn Mawr College Special Collections.

"Imperial Instructions (*goshinyu*)" issued by the Meiji Emperor at the time of the establishment of Peeresses' School regarding the school's educational policies (Takahashi 2002, pp. 135–137). The following quotation is taken from the original text:

> The list of Peeresses' School regulations was reviewed and nothing objectionable was found. Given the urgency expressed by the Minister of the Imperial Household, the item was promptly returned. However, upon further consideration, it was realized that there is a section on chemistry and science [*kagaku rigaku*] in the curriculum book, which was identical to the rules and regulations of the Women's Normal School. Teaching these subjects to girls who will marry into other families, serve their husbands, and manage households goes against the purpose of the girls' school annexed to the Imperial Household. If the school adopts this curriculum, in 5 or 7 years, during the third or fourth year of the Meiji era, the

> graduates will be highly educated and lofty women who are only proficient in chemistry and science. However, they may lack the practical skills necessary for household management, which could be a significant concern. Like the reserve officers' academies, which rise and then suddenly fall into disuse, this should have been considered at inception. Therefore, subjects for girls should include Japanese, Chinese, Western studies, and sewing. (Kaigo 1981, pp. 185–186)

In short, since the girls of the nobility would eventually marry into other families, serve their husbands, and govern their families, they should be educated in practical subjects that were appropriate to their position. The school should therefore not place much emphasis on "lofty" studies. In particular, the natural sciences were not necessary for the education of noblewomen, and they were encouraged to avoid this type of education. Education for girls should differ from education for boys, and this difference should be kept in mind when designing educational programs. At that time, "imperial instructions" had a strong binding force.[6] Umeko could not have been unaware of this instruction. After all, she was sent from this royal school to one of the most advanced women's colleges in the United States, where she defied the imperial edict by majoring in the "forbidden" natural sciences. This was symbolic of her independent spirit and determination.

6 According to Senju Katsumi, the Emperor played a significant role in shaping the direction of national education in the 1880s, and although advice was given by Motoda Nagazane (1818–1891, draftsman of the Imperial Rescript on Education), "The subordinationist view of girls' education expressed by the highest authority is even more significant when considering the importance of the Emperor in the Meiji era" (Senju 1967, p. 26).

Umeko studied at Bryn Mawr for a year and a half before ostensibly spending "one semester" (six months) studying at the Oswego Normal School on Lake Ontario. She intended to study teaching methods during her last semester, which was the original purpose of her studies according to her application. In fact, she only stayed in Oswego for six weeks. The rest of the semester appears to have been spent visiting other universities and elementary schools, according to the manuscript of a lecture that Umeko prepared after returning to Japan:

> I was at Bryn Mawr Women's College for two and a half years in the US, and for six months I walked around visiting primary schools. I also visited Harvard University Women's College, Wellesley College for Women, and elementary schools to see their educational methods. I also spent six weeks at the famous Oswego Normal School in the eastern United States. (untitled Romanized manuscript, Tsuda University Archives)

In the archives of the Oswego Normal School, which are in the Special Collections of the State University of New York at Oswego, there is a handwritten record of Umeko's attendance at "Elementary B," a program on elementary school education methods, during the spring semester beginning in early February and ending in late June, 1891. Unlike the other students, however, there is no credit given for Umeko, suggesting that she did not attend the entire program.[7]

---

7 "Summary of Reports of the Superintendents and Teachers for the term ending June 30, 1891," Special Collections, New York State University, Oswego.

Before leaving Bryn Mawr, Frederic Lee wrote a letter to Umeko confirming her studies at Bryn Mawr:

> Miss Ume Tsuda has taken one year and a half of biological study in Bryn Mawr College. The first, or minor, year consisted of five lectures and six hours of laboratory work per week and was conducted jointly by Professor E. B. Wilson and myself. A series of animal and vegetable forms was carefully studied anatomically and physiologically, the subject being to gain a knowledge of the laws of biology in general and the morphological and physiological relationships of the various animal and plant groups to each other. During the second, or major, year, of which Miss Tsuda has finished one half, she has taken with me a course of two lectures per week with laboratory work, on the comparative anatomy of the vertebrate. This has comprised a much more special study of the vertebrated animals than was possible during the minor year. In all her work with me, Miss Tsuda has shown seriousness, maturity, marked intelligence, and scientific ability. Her course has been one of credit to herself and I regret that she is not able to remain and complete the biological work of the major year. (February 27, 1891, Tsuda University Archives)

In June, just before her promised two-year period of study expired, she requested an extension of one year from the Peeresses' School. Her request for an extension, dated June 15, 1891 (Imperial Household Archives), states that she would be able to "graduate" if she studied at Bryn Mawr College for one more year and that she would like the extension because it would be very relevant to her teaching at the Peeresses' School after her return (Figure 2.10). Her area of study at

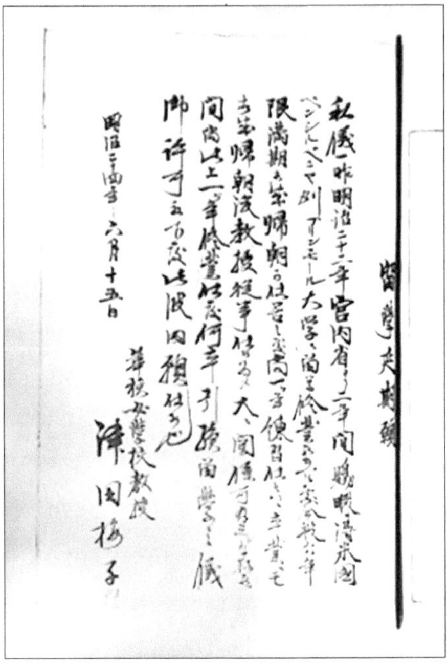

Figure 2.10 Umeko's "Application for Extension of Study," June 15, 1891. Courtesy Imperial Household Archives.

Bryn Mawr is not mentioned. Since it usually took four years to graduate from Bryn Mawr College, the term "graduation" seems like a temporary excuse. In her heart, Umeko knew that if she stayed one more year, she would be able to complete most of the specialized courses in the biology program.

Her request for an extension was approved, but a new condition was added: to "investigate women's education" in the US. This time, she was put on a leave of absence without pay for one year, with a 300-yen allowance.[8] Accordingly, Umeko's academic journey at Bryn Mawr College resumed

8 Kitazawa Masanari to the principal of Peeresses' School and others, June 22, 1891, Gakushuin Archives.

successfully. This pivotal step not only facilitated her continued pursuit of education but also paved the way for her future endeavors in biology.

Chapter 3

Becoming a Biologist

> There are no women in Japan today who are scholars. I do not know whether I have such qualities or not, whether I am capable of drastic research or not, or whether it is my mission to become a scholar or not. However, I would like to more or less develop my innate talents. I should not be prohibited from studying because I am a woman.
>
> – Tsuda Umeko, cited in Yoshikawa Toshikazu, *Tsuda Umeko den*, 1956

> When I had a chance to talk with Morgan about Miss Tsuda, he recalled her personality and ability, asserting in his characteristic way that she attained such achievement and fame simply because she had gotten rid of biology completely.
>
> – Komai Taku, "T. H. Morgan's Times," 1967

Following the approval of an extension to her studies in the United States, Tsuda Umeko advanced her education in the field of biology. Under the guidance of an emerging biologist who had recently joined the Bryn Mawr College faculty, Umeko transitioned from student to researcher. Having won the trust of the college, she was challenged by a pending deadline for her study abroad program. In this chapter, I explore Umeko's thought processes by delving into her relationship with biology during her study and her experiences after returning to Japan.

I also examine the impact of her overseas study experience on her subsequent career trajectory.

A Summer in Woods Hole

From July to August 1891, Umeko attended a summer course at the Woods Hole Marine Biological Laboratory on Cape Cod, Massachusetts, facing the Atlantic Ocean.[1] It is unknown how Umeko travelled to Woods Hole, but at the time it was at least two hours by train from Boston or about 15 hours by sea from New York City (Oshima 1950, p. 263).

The laboratory had opened in 1888, headed by Charles Otis Whitman (1842–1910). Whitman had visited Japan as a hired foreign teacher on the recommendation of Edward Sylvester Morse (1838–1925), the first professor of the Department of Zoology at the University of Tokyo, whom he had succeeded as a professor (1879–1881). He was concurrently a professor at Clark University. He would serve as director of the Woods Hole Marine Biological Laboratory for 20 years until his resignation in 1908, developing the station into a world-class marine biology research center (Kihara et al. (eds.) 1988, pp. 94–99; Watanabe Masao 1976b, pp. 274–298). The seaside summer course was, atypical for the era, open to women researchers, teachers, and students, as the program was funded and requested by the Women's Education Association of Boston (Lillie 1944; Pauly 1988; Rossiter 1982, pp. 86–87).

That year was the institute's fourth summer course, with 44 students participating, about a half of whom were women.

1 The original name of the laboratory was Woods Holl Marine Biological Laboratory, but Holl was later spelled Hole.

Figure 3.1 Woods Hole Marine Biological Laboratory facilities, c.1890. Courtesy Woods Hole Marine Biological Laboratory Archives.

Figure 3.2 The faculty and students of the 1891 summer course. Umeko is not in this photograph. Front row, right (man seated with hat in hand) is Watase Shozaburo, left (bearded figure in white jacket, seated facing right) is Morgan. The elderly man with white hair, almost in the center of the photo, is the director Whitman. Left of him, and slightly behind, is Ida Hyde (in white). To the right of him (also in white) is Bryn Mawr College student Anne Evans. Courtesy Woods Hole Marine Biological Laboratory Archives.

Umeko's name is included in the institute's report. She, along with two other Bryn Mawr students, Anne Evans and Elizabeth Cooke, were selected by the college to participate (The Marine Biological Laboratory 1891, pp. 7–8). For seven weeks, scholars gave a variety of lectures on zoology and

Figure 3.3 Practical training scene. Female students on a summer course at the Woods Hole Marine Biological Laboratory. Although this photograph was taken in 1895, Umeko and other students likely engaged in similar practices. Courtesy Woods Hole Marine Biological Laboratory Archives.

Figure 3.4 Practical training scene, 1896. Courtesy Woods Hole Marine Biological Laboratory Archives.

botany, as well as practical exercises in collecting samples and using microscopes. Lectures were given in the mornings and evenings, and practical work was done in between. The course was a valuable hands-on fieldwork experience for aspiring biologists. Wilson and Morgan lectured at the Woods Hole course that year. It seems that Umeko first met Morgan here, before he took up a position at Bryn Mawr College that fall. Watase Shozaburo (1863–1929) also gave a lecture, so Umeko must have talked to her heart's content with this Japanese zoologist of almost the same age. Watase had studied at Johns Hopkins' Graduate School in 1886 and received a doctorate in 1890 for his dissertation, "On the Morphology of the Compound Eyes of Arthropods." He and Morgan were colleagues at the same university. At that time, Watase was an assistant professor at Clark University, and later an assistant professor at the University of Chicago. In 1901, he would become a professor in the Department of Biology, Tokyo Imperial University (see Mizoguchi 2001a; Kihara et al. (eds.) 1988, pp. 137–141; Miyoshi 1938, pp. 532–545).

The Woods Hole Marine Biological Laboratory is one of the most influential centers for the advancement of biology in the United States. More than 30 people involved in research and education at Woods Hole have received Nobel Prizes. Noguchi Hideyo (1876–1928), a prominent Japanese bacteriologist at the Rockefeller Institute, spent time there during the summers of 1902, 1907, and 1916 studying snake venom. In the 1930s, Dan Katsuma (1904–1996), a Japanese embryologist and cell biologist, also frequently visited. To date, approximately 180 Japanese researchers have studied there. Umeko was the second Japanese researcher to visit Woods Hole, following Watase, who had attended the summer course the previous year (Mizoguchi 2001b, 2002, 2005; Nakazawa 1988).

Research with Morgan

After an impactful summer experience, Umeko returned to Bryn Mawr for the fall semester. Morgan, who would be Umeko's supervisor beginning that semester, was an up-and-coming zoologist who, like Watase, had received his doctorate from Johns Hopkins University in 1890. He was only 25 years old, two years younger than Umeko. He had been invited to replace Wilson, who had moved to Columbia University, as an associate professor on Wilson's strong recommendation.

More than forty years later, in 1933, Morgan would win the Nobel Prize in Physiology or Medicine for his work on mutations. However, it was not until he moved to Columbia University at Wilson's invitation that he shifted his focus to genetics. During his time at Bryn Mawr College (1891–1904), he exclusively worked on embryology. When he collaborated with Umeko, he had just started a new wave of research on experimental embryology. Since his dissertation research on the development of sea spiders, he had been involved in studies on the development of gibbous beetles, several species of fish, starfish, sea urchins, etc (see Boring 1946; Sturtevant 1959; Allen 1970b; Shine and Wrobel 1976; Oppenheimer1983; Kohler 1994).[2]

During his 13 years at Bryn Mawr, Morgan supervised more than 40 research students, but Umeko was the first (Sturtevant 1959). Jane M. Oppenheimer (1911–1996), an embryologist and historian of science who wrote an article on Morgan's research and educational activities at Bryn Mawr, noted that "he clearly respected the intelligence and abilities of his young women students and successfully encouraged them to develop as true scientists" (1983, p. 853). Morgan seems to have taken an immediate liking to Umeko. According to Komai (1886–

2 Morgan's personal papers (Thomas Hunt Morgan Papers) are preserved in the California Institute of Technology Archives, where he worked in later years. However, the archives do not contain any correspondence between Morgan and Umeko.

Figure 3.5 Thomas Hunt Morgan in 1891, when he supervised Umeko's research. Courtesy Woods Hole Marine Biological Laboratory Archives.

Figure 3.6 Morgan (right) on the Bryn Mawr College campus, 1898. Courtesy Bryn Mawr College Special Collections.

1972, a geneticist who studied under Morgan at Columbia University and later became a professor at Kyoto University), he praised Umeko as "a very good student, and her English, of course, was not so different from that of American women students" (Komai 1947, p. 85; 1967).[3]

In the fall semester, Umeko took Morgan's "Post-Major Biology." This was one of those special studies that only students deemed to have outstanding abilities could take,

3 Edwin Grant Conklin, a zoologist, also praised Umeko's English language skills. Oshima Hiroshi wrote about an episode when he visited Conklin's house: "I believe his daughter, who is a student at Smith College, was there too and we had a really nice evening talking. Conklin had nothing but nice things to say about Miss Tsuda Umeko. He said her English was better and more correct than the English spoken by the girls around here. He pointed to the daughter and her friends" (1950, p. 308).

the equivalent of a senior thesis today. She was tasked with observing the cleavage of frog eggs. Frogs' eggs were easy to handle and were commonly used for experimental embryological research at the time. The following spring, 1892, Umeko wrote up the results and submitted the manuscript to Morgan (Tsuda University Archives). The study was so noteworthy that it was featured in the *President's Report to the Board of Trustees*, which stated, "Miss Tsuda's work on the orientation of the axis of the frog's eggs should, on account of its excellence, have special mention" (Bryn Mawr College 1892b, p. 38). In 1894, two years after Umeko returned to Japan, a paper entitled "The Orientation of the Frog's Egg," co-authored by Morgan and Umeko, was published in a British journal, the *Quarterly Journal of Microscopical Science*. Morgan would write more than 170 papers throughout his life, but this was his first co-authored paper.

Thus, while Yasui Kono (1880–1971) has frequently been recognized as the first Japanese woman to publish a paper in a foreign journal, this is incorrect; Yasui's English paper was first published in *the Annals of Botany* in England in 1911, 17 years after Umeko's paper (Yasui 1911; Miyake and Yasui 1911; cf. Kagawa Jinken Kenkyusho 2006, p.15; Saijo 2009, p. 156; Miki 2004, p. 8).[4] It is highly probable that Umeko was the first Japanese woman to publish a research paper in natural science in a foreign journal.

The July 1894 issue of a women's magazine, *Jogaku Zasshi*, published a short report titled "The Biological Discovery of Miss Tsuda Ume," which stated:

---

4 Yasui took a summer course at the Woods Hole Marine Biological Laboratory in 1915 (16 years after Umeko) (Mizoguchi 2001b, p. 16).

> This experiment is the research that she conducted at Bryn Mawr College for Women. While it is documented that Dr. Morgan provided assistance, the initial discovery was made by herself. German scholars such as [Eduard Friedrich Wilhelm] Pflüger [1829–1910] and Roux are working on similar research. But she finally made a valuable discovery that enriched the academic study of the subject. It was accomplished by the power of the Japanese woman. (p. 693)

This report appears to be based on information provided by Umeko herself, who was a frequent contributor to *Jogaku Zasshi*. If so, her pride in her research is evident in the text.

The paper consists of Morgan's introduction at the beginning, Umeko's research on "Normal development and location of blastopore," and Morgan's research on "Results obtained by injury to definite portions of the early embryo" and "Results obtained from embryos whose development had been modified by artificial means," and finally Morgan's conclusion. It is a comparative study of normal and abnormal development using the methods of experimental embryology. Morgan's experiment on abnormal development was conducted in the spring of 1893, after Umeko returned to Japan, and was integrated with Umeko's research on normal development, which had been completed before her departure. In the controversy over the location of frog embryo formation (whether embryos form in the black hemisphere, which has many pigment granules, or in the white hemisphere), their results differed from previous studies by Roux and others. But the more essential finding, pointed out by Nakazawa Shingo (1918–2002), was that the left and right sides of the tadpole's body are already determined at the first division of the egg,

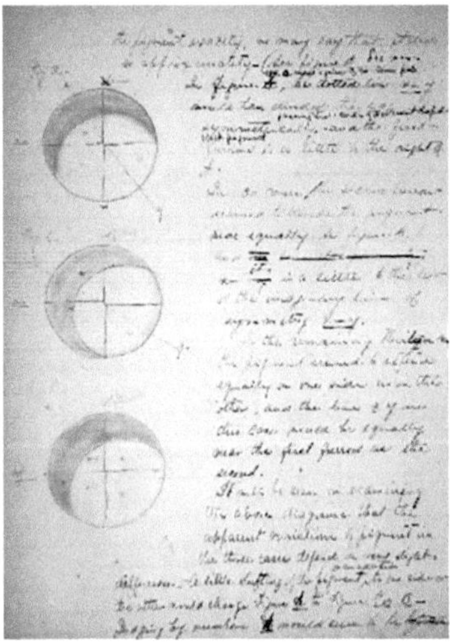

Figure 3.7 Umeko's manuscript for the paper. Courtesy Tsuda University Archives.

Figure 3.8 Paper with Morgan, "The Orientation of the Frog's Egg" (1894). Photo by the author.

confirming that the first division plane of the embryo in frog egg division corresponds to the median plane through which the left and right sides of the later-developing embryo are centered (Nakazawa 1988, p. 47).

Although this paper may not stand out among Morgan's vast and spectacular achievements in biology, it is worth noting that it was a significant contribution to the emerging field of experimental embryology, as evidenced by his reference to it in his 1897 monograph, *The Development of the Frog's Egg: An Introduction to Experimental Embryology* (p. 158).

The faculty members at the department all agreed that Umeko was a bright, capable, and hardworking student. She was older and more grounded than average American students, and they looked up to her. Table 3.1 shows the number of students enrolled in courses in the Department of Biology at that time. We can see that the number of students increased

Table 3.1 Course Enrollment in the Department of Biology at Bryn Mawr College

Academic Year	1888–1889	1889–1890	1890–1891	1891–1892	1892–1893
Undergraduate students (cumulative total number)	23	23	26	37	38
(1) Minor Courses	16	20	17	27	30
(2) Major Courses	3	3	9	8	5
(3) Post Major Courses	4	0	0	2	3
Graduate students	3	3	2	8	4
Total (cumulative)	26	26	28	45	42
Total (actual)	24	26	28	44	42

Note: Compiled from Bryn Mawr College, *The President's Report to the Board of Trustees*, 1889, 1890, 1891, 1892, 1893. Special students like Umeko are excluded. The cumulative total differs from the actual total because some students took both minor and major courses.

from the fall semester of 1891 to the spring semester of 1892, when Morgan and other new faculty members were brought in. To cope with the influx of students, Umeko was hired as a student-assistant in the biological laboratory, along with Ida Henrietta Hyde (1857–1945). Umeko was responsible for a minor course, "General Biology A" (fall semester, taught by Morgan, Loeb, and Goff), and a laboratory class run in conjunction with "General Biology B" (spring semester, taught by Warren, Loeb, and Keller), and mentored other students.[5]

Hyde attended the summer course at Woods Hole with Umeko in 1891, after graduating from Cornell University. She subsequently worked as an assistant at Bryn Mawr College

5 Bryn Mawr College, *Trustee's Minutes*, dated October 9, 1891 (Bryn Mawr College Library Special Collections), states, "Under the pressure of increasing biology enrollment, it became necessary to hire a Cornell graduate, Ida Hyde, as a laboratory student assistant at a salary of $300 per year. In addition, a

Figure 3.9 Ida Henrietta Hyde, who served as a laboratory assistant together with Umeko at Bryn Mawr College.

Figure 3.10 Umeko in her Bryn Mawr days, age 24. Courtesy Tsuda University Archives.

and received her doctorate in physiology from the University of Heidelberg, Germany, in 1896. While at Bryn Mawr, she served as Loeb's assistant. She was the first woman to study at Harvard Medical School and later became a professor at the University of Kansas. Even in the US, the scientific world at that time was still dominated by men, and Hyde is widely recognized today as the epitome of an early woman scientist who struggled to make ends meet. Her unpublished autobiography, "Before Women Were Human Beings: A Woman from the Dark Ages," describes her hardships (American Association of University Women Archives; cf. Hyde 1938; Rossiter 1982, pp. 41–43). She later visited Umeko's Joshi

Japanese student, Ume Tsuda, was hired as a second assistant at a total cost of $50." See also Bryn Mawr College 1892b, p. 37.

Eigaku Juku in Tokyo and acknowledged Umeko's contribution to the improvement of women's education in Japan (paper, Ida Hyde Collection, Marine Biological Laboratory Library).

Struggles and Return Home

Umeko's transcripts are impressive. She took most of the subjects in the biology curriculum at the forefront of the nation's higher education and excelled.[6] Moreover, hers was a more in-depth study of biology than most of the undergraduates at Bryn Mawr (see Chapter 5), and Umeko was invited to remain at the college to continue her studies. The offer was probably made by Dean Thomas, who had heard about Umeko's talent from Morgan and other faculty members. Bryn Mawr was the first college in the country to offer fellowships to women. If she had remained at Bryn Mawr, she would have been a fellowship student and would have been on track to receive her doctorate from Morgan.

However, after much consideration, Umeko declined the offer. According to a memorandum by Anna Cope Hartshorne (1860–1957), a Bryn Mawr friend of Umeko's who later visited Japan to support Umeko's English school, the Bryn Mawr College officials were "amazed, incredulous, and then indignant" when they heard her reply. Hartshorne continues, "I don't believe Miss Thomas ever quite forgave her what probably seems ingratitude and misprizing of true scholarship." Hartshorne also says that this was the only "shortsighted"

---

6 Umeko's transcripts give her a grade of H (High Credit) for many of her credit courses. Bryn Mawr College Record of Ume Tsuda, Tsuda University Archives; Umé Tsuda, Transcript, 1889–1892, Bryn Mawr College Special Collections.

decision Umeko ever made in her life, because it was an attractive offer, which was rarely made even to Americans at the time (Hartshorne memorandum, Dec. 13, 1933, Tsuda University Archives; cf. Hartshorne 1929, pp. 513–514). Given Morgan's subsequent transition from embryology to genetics and his successful career at Bryn Mawr College, Columbia University, and the California Institute of Technology, where he mentored numerous gifted students, this offer was a once-in-a-lifetime, golden opportunity for a future research career. Bryn Mawr professors praised Umeko's talent as a researcher and said that if she had continued her studies, she would have had great success in the scientific community (Hartshorne memorandum, n.d., Tsuda University Archives; Thomas May 27, 1892, Bryn Mawr College Special Collection).

The difference between US and Japanese university degrees was significant. It was more than 30 years later, in 1927, that Yasui Kono became Japan's first female doctor of science (in biology at Tokyo Imperial University). Umeko's student Nakanishi Fumiko wrote, "If she had remained a scholar, Japan would have had a woman doctor of science before Dr. Yasui Konoko" (1929, p. 103), which is probably right.

Of course, Umeko had wavered. Yoshikawa states:

> It appeared that [at Bryn Mawr] she had become completely immersed in biological experiments, both physically and mentally. Even then, however, Umeko could not make up her mind to become a scientist in the future. Therein lay Umeko's hesitation. She had no intention of spending the rest of her life as an English teacher. But it would be difficult for her to become a biologist. Her circumstances also did not allow her to do so. (1956, p. 235)

Umeko's decision, which was difficult for Americans such as Thomas, Hartshorn, and Morgan to understand, must be considered from her position as a Japanese government-sponsored student of this period. Umeko's purpose in studying abroad this time was, ostensibly, to acquire teaching skills in English education. She wanted to use this knowledge for the education of girls in Japan, and for the time being, for English education at the Peeresses' School. After all, the government had funded her salary for the first two years of her studies and granted her an additional year to complete them. She had a sense of duty to serve upon her return to Japan. The Peeresses' School took this as a matter of course. Umeko's morals apparently would not allow her to be so individualistic as to stay in the US and continue her study of biology after the government had paid for her to study abroad twice, for a total of 14 years. The rare opportunity by the government to study abroad as a woman had been given to Umeko as a member of the Meiji elite, and as such, she could not disregard the shackles of the state. Throughout her life, she was acutely aware of her self-imposed duty to contribute to the "modernization" of the nation.

Even if Umeko had returned to Japan to continue her studies in biology, it would have been nearly impossible for her to find employment in that field. At that time, it was almost impossible for women in Japan to become scientists. Imperial universities (*teikoku daigaku*, national universities in the prewar Japan) had long been men's schools. Tohoku Imperial University was the first imperial university to admit three women, Tange Ume (1873–1955, chemistry), Kuroda Chika (1884–1968, chemistry), and Kanayama (née Makita) Raku (1888–1977, mathematics), and that was not until 1913

(Yukawa 2003, pp. 50–72), nearly a quarter of a century after Umeko matriculated at Bryn Mawr. When Umeko returned to Japan, there were almost no scientific research positions available for women.

Besides, Umeko had a different path in mind. She had been planning to establish a private school for women's higher education when she returned to Japan. She had a budding sense of mission to free Japanese women from ignorance through a private school education – freed from the constraints on a government school such as Peeresses' – and to do her utmost to improve the status of women.

Umeko's deadline for studying in the US was at the end of the spring semester, in May 1892, but her father Sen requested an extension of three more months to return to Japan from the Peeresses' School, which was granted (Tsuda Sen May 27, 1892, Gakushuin Archives). With Mrs. Morris' encouragement, she devoted the remainder of her stay to raising funds from American women for a scholarship for Japanese women. She returned to Japan on August 12 and resumed her position at Peeresses' School in September. She was 27 years old at the time.

After returning to Japan, Umeko did not speak much in public about her study of biology. However, her continued interest in biology can be seen in several letters she exchanged with Morgan (preserved in the Tsuda University Archives). In a letter dated July 25, 1893, Umeko expressed nostalgia for her studies at Bryn Mawr and Woods Hole and confirmed that her interest in the subject had not waned. She also revealed that, upon her return to Japan, she had continued to engage in research, albeit in a different manner. She indicated that she had preserved frog eggs and continued to observe their development. In her observations of embryos, she identified a late stage of division that deviated from the standard. She consulted with Professor Mitsukuri of Imperial University, who stated that this was distinct from any other amphibians he had observed. Due to her engagement with other matters, she was unable to proceed with this research. Therefore, she said she would transmit the material to Morgan, requesting that he examine it and provide her with his assessment.

In a letter dated in October 14, 1893, Morgan responded to Umeko's letter as follows:

> The materials were received in good condition. As your research seems to be very promising, I suggest that you continue to observe the egg breaking and embryo formation until the next spring. The Biology Department at Bryn Mawr College is in a state of continuous development. We often speak of you & always with the wish that you will come back to America before long. (Tsuda University Archives)

The construction of Dalton Hall on the university's campus was finalized that year. This building was designated for use by the Biology Department and boasted significantly improved facilities.[7]

The Mitsukuri Umeko mentioned was Mitsukuri Kakichi (1858–1909), professor of biology at the Imperial University. He went to the US in 1873 at the age of 15, studied at Yale University, and then at Johns Hopkins University Graduate School from 1879 to 1880 under Brooks, where he was a

7 The splendor of Dalton Hall is described in a letter from Leah Goff to Umeko (dated January 24, 1893, Tsuda University Archives) just before the opening.

fellow from 1880–1881. He received his Ph.D. in 1883. He was an alumnus of Wilson at Johns Hopkins. Wilson was Bryn Mawr's first biology professor and had taught Umeko. Mitsukuri had encouraged Watase Shozaburo to study at Johns Hopkins University. In 1882, Mitsukuri became the third professor of Zoology appointed in the Department of Biology at the University of Tokyo, succeeding Morse and Whitman. In 1886, he founded the Misaki Marine Biological Station (attached to the Imperial University) at the southwestern tip of the Miura Peninsula in Kanagawa Prefecture (see Tamaki 1998; Mizoguchi 1999, 2001a; Kihara et al. (eds.) 1988, pp.100–106).[8]

Umeko had known Mitsukuri personally before her second trip to the US. They had performed "The Merchant of Venice" together as members of an English-language theater club established by Sutematsu in 1883. The club also included Sakurai Joji (1858–1939), a chemist at the University of Tokyo, and Takamine Hideo's wife (Kuno 1993a, p. 164; Sutematz letter to Alice Bacon, January 18, 1883, Oyama Collection, Vassar College Libraries). It is not clear to what extent Umeko and Mitsukuri were connected prior to her second study abroad, but it is not difficult to imagine that Wilson mentioned to her that Mitsukuri was a close friend. In any case, it is evident that Mitsukuri was one of the few people Umeko consulted in her biological research after returning to Japan.

---

8 Kameda 2005 (p.139) has incorrectly identified the Mitsukuri in Umeko's letter as "Mitsukuri Genpachi" (1862–1919), Kakichi's younger brother. Although Genpachi studied zoology at the University of Tokyo, he had switched to history by then because he was extremely nearsighted and could not use a microscope.

Figure 3.11 Mitsukuri Kakichi. In 1881, Mitsukuri became the first Japanese professor of zoology at the University of Tokyo, succeeding Whitman. *Dobutsugaku Zasshi* 1910.

Letters exchanged between Mitsukuri and Umeko are stored in the Tsuda University Archives. These letters, written in English, corroborate the letter to Morgan cited above. In a letter dated March 25, 1893, Mitsukuri stated that Umeko had asked him to order reagents, including alcohol and picric acid, as well as 30 specimen bottles and 10 eye dishes. He also noted that his fellow researcher Ishikawa Chiyomatsu (1861–1935) resided near Umeko's residence in Takehaya-cho, Koishikawa-ku, Tokyo, and that Ishikawa had his students assist her in collecting frogs and their eggs. Mitsukuri encouraged Umeko to persevere in her research endeavors. Ishikawa published *Dobutsu shinka-ron* [Animal Evolution Theory] (1883), a transcription of Morse's lectures, and was a prominent popularizer of evolutionary theory in Japan. He was a professor at the Imperial University Faculty of Agriculture and president of Tokyo Zoological Society (Tokyo Dobutsu

Gakkai). He was a disciple of Whitman and was interested in embryology (Kihara et al. (eds.) 1988, pp. 126–130; *Dobutsugaku Zasshi* 1935). Umeko responded to Mitsukuri, thanking him for his encouragement, and assuring him that she would resume her research and continue to ask for his advice (Tsuda University Archives). Mitsukuri published "A New Division of Zoology," in *Toyo Gakugei Zasshi* in 1898, in which he discussed the rise of experimental embryology and favorably introduced Morgan's recent research on frog egg splitting as an example, saying that Morgan "discovered very interesting facts." However, he introduced it as the research of "Mr. Morgan of the US" and did not mention Umeko.

This was two decades after Morse and Whitman had introduced modern Western zoology in the Department of Biology at the University of Tokyo's Faculty of Science in 1877. Mitsukuri succeeded them upon his return from the US, and Iijima Isao (1861–1921) was hired upon his return from Germany in 1886. Because of the two professors' specialties, almost all students were biased toward zoology and none majored in botany (Yatsu 1939; Isono 1985; Mizoguchi 2001a). By 1893, 16 students had graduated. However, none focused on subjects outside of taxonomy, morphology, or descriptive embryology. Mitsukuri understood the importance of experimental methods but had not yet introduced them to education and research. It was not until Yatsu Naohide (1876–1947), who studied under Wilson and Morgan at Columbia University, took over the position in 1907 that experimental research began to take off in earnest (Fukui 2000; Mizoguchi 2001a).

In 1878, Morse advocated for the establishment of the University of Tokyo Society of Biology. The society temporarily ceased activities during Whitman's tenure. Mitsukuri rebuilt it in 1882, renaming it the Tokyo Society of Biology (Tokyo Seibutsu Gakkai). Three years later, it split in two: one for plants and one for animals, creating the Tokyo Zoological Society (Tokyo Dobutsu Gakkai). Its journal, *Dobutsugaku Zasshi* (Zoological Journal), published its first issue in 1888, just before Umeko enrolled at Bryn Mawr. At the time, however, it was not a journal for professional researchers; instead, it focused on articles that promoted zoology for primary and secondary education teachers and general readers (Hayashi 2000, 2001). At the time, Japan was in the process of adopting Western biology through trial and error, both in terms of system and scientific content. This was quite different from the established academic institutions in Europe and the United States. Under these circumstances, Umeko did not engage with the Japanese academic community, except for personal interactions with some zoologists, such as Mitsukuri.

Anna Hartshorne, however, wrote that Umeko had a lingering desire for science. When Umeko founded Joshi Eigaku Juku, she had intended to establish a science department, although her plans are unclear. She continued to subscribe to scientific journals and books until she realized that financial considerations made this impossible (Hartshorne memoranda, Dec. 13, 1933, and Nov. 16, 1940, Tsuda University Archives).

In May 1898, at the urging of Oyama Sutematsu, Umeko was appointed to concurrently serve as a professor of English at the Women's Higher Normal School. Uryu Shigeko was a professor of music at the school. The previous year, the school had established a department of science (Rika) and an advanced program. This was the first time that science education was offered to women in tertiary education. At the same time, Iwakawa Tomotaro (1855–1933) was hired as a full-time biology professor. Iwakawa was one of the first graduates of the Department of Biology at the University of Tokyo and had studied zoology with Morse and Whitman. All science education posts at the Women's Higher Normal School were occupied by men (Tokyo Joshi Koto Shihan Gakko (ed.) 1898–1900, pp. 133–136). Yasui Kono enrolled at the school that year and eventually proceeded into the advanced program, where she researched carp organs under Iwakawa (cf. Yasui 1905). Umeko was at the school only for two years, and it is unclear whether she had any contact with Iwakawa.

Farewell to Biology

As Umeko devoted her energies to creating a school for women, she gradually moved away from biology. In September 1900, she realized her dream by opening Joshi Eigaku Juku (Women's School for English Studies). In her later years, Umeko said, "I want my Juku to be a true *daigaku* [university/college]" (Katayama 1929, p. 138). Bryn Mawr College might have been the prototype of the daigaku she aspired to establish. Umeko had her students at Joshi Eigaku Juku study physiology and encouraged them to observe plants and animals, which may have been the least she could do (see Chapter 5; Tsuda Juku Rika no rekishi wo kisoku suru kai (ed.) 1987, p. 144).

Umeko was repeatedly in and out of the hospital from around 1917 with diabetes and several cerebral hemorrhages, and passed away in the summer of 1929. Several years before she passed away, Yoshikawa Toshikazu, a staff member of

Joshi Eigaku Juku, began working on Umeko's biography. Umeko cooperated from her sickbed, providing materials, and writing to Morgan, who had moved to Columbia University, asking him to send a reprint of their joint paper if he had one. Morgan replied that unfortunately there were no reprints left. The letter concludes with the following words: "What a great person you have become to have your biography written! But I am not surprised" (February 4, 1926, Tsuda University Archives). A year after Umeko's death, Yoshikawa completed a biography about Tsuda Umeko. Three years later, in 1933, Morgan was awarded the Nobel Prize in Physiology or Medicine.

Morgan sarcastically observed that Umeko's achievements and fame were only possible because she had completely abandoned biology (Komai 1967, p. 247).[9] After Umeko returned to Japan, Morgan married Lilian V. Sampson (1870–1952), a graduate student he had supervised at Bryn Mawr. They got married in 1904, when he moved to Columbia University.[10] At Columbia, he shifted his research focus from embryology to genetics from about 1908. He was awarded the Nobel Prize for his "discovery of the genetic function of chromosomes;" he drew a chromosome map based on his studies of mutations in *Drosophila*, which showed that genes are located on chromosomes in the cell. Since Gregor Johann Mendel (1822–1884), the gene had been an abstract concept.

---

9 Komai also wrote, Morgan "knew that she had returned home and built a fine school, and joked that 'it was because she had abandoned zoology altogether, and she would never be able to do so if she continued to study zoology'" (1947, p. 84).

10 Lilian Morgan continued her research in embryology and genetics after her marriage (Keenan 1983).

Morgan's confirmation of the gene as a material entity on a chromosome set the course for subsequent genetic research. His students included the Nobel Prize winners in Physiology or Medicine: Hermann Joseph Muller (1890–1967), George Well Beadle (1903–1989), and Max Ludwig Henning Delbrück (1906–1981). This legacy serves as a testament to his establishment of a distinct research tradition within the field (Allen 1970b; Waller 2017). It is worth reiterating that Morgan's achievements in genetics built upon his earlier studies in experimental embryology at Bryn Mawr, and his first experimental partner was Umeko.

It was not merely personal interest that led Umeko to pursue biology at Bryn Mawr, if only briefly. It was also a response to a challenge of her times, when it was almost impossible for a woman to be a scientist. By doing in America what she could not do in Japan, she challenged the taboo against Japanese women and proved that it was actually possible for a woman to contribute to scientific research. When Umeko left Peeresses' School to establish her own school, she wrote to President M. Carey Thomas, a respected feminist, saying, she decided to break off "from the red-tape and conservatism which must surround a school like the Peeresses' School" (Letter dated August 9, 1900, Bryn Mawr College Library Special Collections). This was a stance analogous to her father's, as Sen was likewise out of power and opposed to the status quo.

Umeko founded a private school to provide authentic education in English for women. She often said that English was not the end goal. She believed that teaching English to Japanese women would open their eyes to the Western world, thought, and science, which would in turn lead to an awareness of the existence of gender, or social inequality, among Japanese women. These Meiji Enlightenment-inspired ideas were germinated in her teaching experience in Japan after her first period of studying abroad and transformed into an unshakable belief based on her later experience at Bryn Mawr College. It was consolidated through her study of biology, a natural science that in Japan was considered a "lofty" discipline ill-suited to women. For Umeko, the study of biology was integral to her career as a feminist and an educator of women.

Chapter 4

Behind the Scenes at Joshi Eigaku Juku

Japan cannot truly take a high stand until the women, as well as the men, are educated.

– Tsuda Umeko,
"The Education of Japanese Women," 1891

In pursuing a special course of study, one is apt to study narrow. In learning one thing well, we are apt to lose our hold of other things. In taking this special English course, and while endeavoring to perfect yourselves in this branch, do not neglect other things, which go on to make up the complete woman; endeavor daily to keep yourselves informed of general matters, and to be in touch with other lines of work.

– Tsuda Umeko,
speech at the opening ceremony of the Joshi Eigaku Juku, 1900

[My mother] was exceptionally good at mathematics, and for the five years that she was a student at the high school for girls, she was at the top of her class. Her teachers encouraged her parents to send her to Nara Women's Higher Normal School (the predecessor of Nara Women's University) in order to develop her talent. However, my mother gave up the idea of going there in tears because of a comment from an elder relative who said, "Women don't need learning."

– Yonezawa Fumiko,
The Way of Life of Saruhashi Katsuko, 2009

Before World War II, after finishing elementary school (*jinjo shogakko*, usually six years), boys and girls were usually educated separately in Japan. Boys could then go on to junior high school (*chugakko*, five years), high school (*koto gakko*, three years), and university (*daigaku*, three years). For girls, there were two options: either girls' high school (*koto jogakko*, four or five years) or women's normal school (*joshi shihan gakko*, five years). After that, only vocational schools (*senmon gakko*, three or four years) or two women's higher normal schools (*joshi koto shihan gakko*, four years) (Tokyo and Nara) were available. Universities were basically men-only institutions of higher education. It was not until after the war that women were officially granted admission to the university.

Underlying the prewar system was the common belief that women did not need higher learning. In this chapter, we will briefly deviate from the scientific discourse to delve into the historical underpinnings of this belief, tracing its origins back to the Meiji era. We will then proceed to examine the role of Joshi Eigaku Juku (Women's School for English Studies) as a higher education institution for women offering educational programs beyond the secondary level. We will then trace Tsuda Umeko's education during the school's development, the reactions of the students, the relationship and separation between Umeko and the people surrounding the school, and the path leading to Umeko's death.

Arguments against Higher Education for Women

During the Meiji era (1868–1912) and the Taisho era (1912–1926), there were a small number of active male proponents of women's education, including Tsuda Sen, Takamine Hideo, Naruse Jinzo (1958–1919), Iwamoto Yoshiharu (1863–1942), and Nitobe Inazo (1862–1933). At the same time, however, the prevailing argument among educators and policymakers was that higher education was unnecessary for girls. This directly reflected the view of the nation and gender roles under the era's family system. For example, Kikuchi Dairoku (1855–1917), a mathematician who served successively as president of Tokyo Imperial University, president of Kyoto Imperial University, and Minister of Education, made the following comments at a 1902 meeting of the heads of girls' high schools:

> In Japan, a woman's job is not to work independently, but to marry and become a good wife and wise mother. Most girls will do this job in the future. So, girls' education must aim at this end. Advanced studies would help women become independent, but I do not think it necessary to provide them with such studies publicly. (cited in Sakurai 1943, p. 115)

Similarly, at the Japan Association of Women's Education (Dai Nihon Fujin Kyoiku Kai, established in 1887), Kikuchi stated: "At one time the phrase 'equal rights for men and women' was very popular, but I consider such a phrase to be an abhorrent one." He repeated that it was a woman's vocation to marry and become a "good wife and wise mother (*ryosai kenbo*)" (ibid., p. 116).

Figure 4.1 Yamakawa Kenjiro, brother of Sutematsu, physicist, and educator. He served as president of Tokyo Imperial University, Kyoto Imperial University, and Kyushu Imperial University. Courtesy Kyushu University Archives.

Sutematsu's older brother, Yamakawa Kenjiro, a physicist who served as president of Tokyo Imperial University, advanced the argument that higher education was extremely disadvantageous for women. Yamakawa at an extraordinary educational conference in 1917 said that higher education would put mental and physical pressure on girls, increase the mortality rate, and reduce fertility. He asserted that education up to high school was sufficient, and that if girls were to receive further higher education, they would fall out of wedlock and hinder the reproduction of the nation:

> The highest rate of pregnancies is for women aged 21 and 22. Higher education would delay their marriages by about three years, which hinders the reproduction of our people…

> It would increase the mortality rate and late-marriage rate of women. This is extremely disadvantageous to our people. (cited in Kaigo (ed.) 1962, p. 763; cf. Yamakawa Kenjiro 1911, 1937, pp. 732–735; Hatanaka 2004, pp. 102–105)

Sutematsu strongly disagreed with her brother on these issues and actively supported Umeko's Joshi Eigaku Juku and other higher education for women based on her own experience.

In 1900, around the time Yoshioka Yayoi (1871–1959) established Tokyo Women's Medical School (Tokyo Joi Gakko, the precursor of Tokyo Women's Medical University) and began training women doctors, the "theory of national ruin caused by women doctors" (*joi bokoku-ron*) emerged. In this context, the "theory that higher education for women is harmful" was again advocated, similar to Yamakawa's. In other words, the provision of higher education to girls would lead them to marry later in life or force them to remain celibate, thereby reducing Japan's population and undermining the national interest. It was also argued that an increase in the number of girls who were accustomed to seeing blood during surgery would have a negative impact on Japanese culture and aesthetic values, and could eventually lead to the nation's downfall. This position considered the medical profession to be incompatible with "women's characteristics" and sought to exclude women (Watanabe Yoko 2014, pp. 123–124).

In her autobiography *Genshi, josei wa taiyo de atta* [Originally, Women Were the Sun], the women's activist Hiratsuka Raicho (Hiratsuka Haru, 1886–1971) commented on a lecture given by Okuma Shigenobu (1838–1922), a former prime minister and patron of the school, when she was a student at Japan Women's University (Nihon Joshi Daigakko, then

Figure 4.2 Hiratsuka Raicho, 1910. Hiratsuka graduated from the School of Home Economics at Japan Women's University in 1906, founded the "Blue Stockings Society" (*Seito-sha*), and published the literary and artistic magazine *Seito* (Blue Stockings) (1911–1916), which was written by women for women. In her later years, she joined the "Committee of Seven to Appeal for World Peace (World Peace 7)" with Yukawa Hideki (1907–1981) and others, and encouraged Saruhashi Katsuko (1920–2007) to launch the Society of Japanese Women Scientists (1958). Courtesy Okumura Naofumi.

a vocational school despite the name). She wrote, in her typical style:

> Leading figures in politics [and business], who are patrons, visited our school and sometimes gave us speeches. However, I was never impressed by their speeches. They were usually just a bunch of stretched-out platitudes with no substance. I never thought of people like that as great or respectable. I was particularly unimpressed by Count Okuma's arrogance. He did not recognize a need to educate women for their own benefit. Rather, he believed that Japan would disgrace itself if women remained stupid as the country rose in power. He believed that if women did not keep pace with men's progress,

> they would hinder Japan's national strength. My jaw dropped when I heard that. (Hiratsuka 1971, p. 151)

Hiratsuka entered Japan Women's University in 1903, inspired by the educational philosophy of its founder, Naruse Jinzo, who advocated the education of girls "as human beings, women, and citizens." For her, Okuma's derogatory remarks about women, delivered in his capacity as the school's founding chairman and trustee, were nothing short of disillusioning.

This suggests that not all educators and politicians who supported women's higher education were motivated by respect for women's personhood and dignity. Even if they recognized women's personhood, many proponents of women's higher education believed that women were essentially maternal and that an education emphasizing human and feminine development was necessary to bring out these characteristics. These views were not limited to male educators, but were shared by female educators such as Shimoda Utako, who was acquainted with Tsuda Umeko and became the principal of Jissen Girls' School (Jissen Jogakko), and Yasui Tetsu (1870–1945), who became the dean and president of Tokyo Woman's Christian University (Tokyo Joshi Daigaku, then a vocational school despite the name). Particularly, Shimoda's position can be understood as a version of "domestic feminism" that linked the ideal of the "good wife and wise mother" with the improvement of women's status (see Hiroi (ed.) 2021; Kagawa 2021; Hiroi 2021).[1] In contrast to the higher education of

1 In contrast, Yasui promoted a Christian-based liberal arts education for the formation of character and was a staunch critic of the Japanese style of "good wife, wise mother" (Aoyama 1949; Miyata 1993). For more on "domestic" feminism, see Imai (ed.) 1992.

men, there was minimal acknowledgement that the education of girls was an opportunity for academic exploration and the development of professional expertise (Yukawa 2003, pp. 342–344).

As discussed in previous chapters, Umeko was raised in a Victorian-era American family and was instilled with its view of family. In this sense, she emphasized the virtues of femininity and the role of women in the home, which differed from the Japanese idea of a good wife and wise mother in support of the patriarchal system. She was strongly opposed to the latter. While at Bryn Mawr College, she was greatly influenced by the views on women's higher education of her feminist mentor, M. Carey Thomas. Although Umeko did not reject the Victorian view of the family as Thomas did, she agreed that the beliefs that "learning is for men" and "science is for men" needed to be overthrown. In a context in which the prevailing views were hostile to higher education for women, Joshi Eigaku Juku was established, as stated in Chapter 1, Article 1 of the school's 1904 regulations, as a school "whose purpose is to teach highly specialized studies to women, with English as the main subject" (Tsuda Juku Daigaku 100 nenshi hensan iinkai (ed.) 2003, p. 50).

Enthusiastic "Dojo (Little Girl)"

In the Japanese language, the term "*juku*" is used to denote a small, private tutoring school. When it first opened in 1900, Umeko's Joshi Eigaku Juku was located, as its name suggests, in a small house in Ichiban-cho, Kojimachi-ward in the center of Tokyo. In 1902 it moved to more spacious facilities in near by Motozon-cho before moving again in 1903 to nearby

Figure 4.3 At the opening of Joshi Eigaku Juku in 1900, with collaborators in establishing the school. From right to left: Oyama Sutematsu, Uryu Shigeko, Alice Bacon, and Umeko. Courtesy Tsuda University Archives.

Goban-cho, where it occupied the facilities recently abandoned by a girls' school. The acquisition of the school buildings and construction of a dormitory were financed by philanthropic donations from American women. In 1904, the school was officially recognized as a "vocational school (*senmon gakko*)" in accordance with the 1903 Vocational School Ordinance (*Senmon Gakko Rei*). Vocational schools in this period were "schools for teaching advanced academic studies" for those who had completed secondary education. The term of study was required to be three years or more (Amano 2009, Ch. 8).

Figure 4.4 Umeko in the year following the opening of the school, 1901. Courtesy Tsuda University Archives.

In the same year, the school was granted incorporated association status by the Minister of Education. In 1905, the school was granted the status of secondary teacher without examination (a privilege that allows graduates to be qualified to teach secondary school English without examination) (Tsuda Eigaku Juku (ed.) 1941, pp. 87–91).[2] Consequently, the number of students jumped from a dozen or so in 1900 to 150 in 1908 (Tsuda Juku Daigaku 100 nenshi hensan iinkai (ed.) 2003, vol. 2, p. 108). Thus, Joshi Eigaku Juku at the Gobancho campus enjoyed steady growth in its first ten years.

In a 1906 guide to women's schools, the newspaper reporter Nakamura Chiyomatsu (1867–1941) wrote: "those who study

2 For more information on the system of qualification for the non-examination of secondary school teachers at womens' vocational schools, see Sasaki 2002, Ch. 1, S. 2.

Figure 4.5 The library of Joshi Eigaku Juku, Goban-cho Campus before the Great Kanto Earthquake. Courtesy Tsuda University Archives.

[at Joshi Eigaku Juku] must have sound minds and a wealth of knowledge to be able to keep pace with the other students…. All the students in the dormitories are too busy reading and studying. In other words, anyone who joins this school must be a thorough reader" (Nakamura Chiyomatsu 1906, p. 37). The guide was written for young women who wanted to enroll in a vocational school in the Tokyo area. It conveys, with some exaggeration, the rigors of study at Umeko's school.

From the beginning, Umeko stressed the importance of acquiring a broad range of education, rather than just specializing in English (Tsuda Juku Daigaku (ed.) 1984, pp. 1–4; cf. Mamatkulova 2011a, 2021). The curriculum was centered on English, but other subjects such as ethics, psychology, education, Japanese, Chinese classics, history, and gymnastics were also offered (Tsuda Juku Daigaku 100 nenshi hensan iinkai (ed.) 2003, vol. 2, p. 52). In

Figure 4.6 Nitobe Inazo, 1902. An agricultural politician and educator, Nitobe was instrumental in founding and running Joshi Eigaku Juku and later served as the first president of Tokyo Woman's Christian University. Courtesy Nitobe Memorial Hall.

addition, special lectures were given every other week as extracurricular classes. For example, Iwamoto Yoshiharu, a student of Tsuda Sen and a friend of Umeko's, and Nitobe Inazo gave some of these lectures. They were well received by the students. Iwamoto, then editor of *Jogaku Zasshi* (first published in 1885) and the principal of Meiji Girl's School (Meiji Jogakko), gave lectures on ethics and morality. Nitobe gave a series of lectures on his bestselling book, *Bushido: The Soul of Samurai*, published in New York in 1899. Iwamoto and Nitobe were both also members of the Incorporated Association Joshi Eigaku Juku (ibid., vol. 1, p. 73).

In the classroom, Umeko's teaching was rigorous and passionate. Yamakawa (née Aoyama) Kikue (1890–1980,

Figure 4.7 Yamakawa Kikue, summer 1920. Yamakawa was a theorist, activist, and critic in the socialist movement. After the war, she became the first director of the Women and Youth Bureau of the Ministry of Labor under the Katayama Cabinet. Courtesy Yamakawa Kikue Kinenkai (Yamakawa Kikue Memorial Association).

graduated in 1912) learned English from Umeko at Joshi Eigaku Juku. She wrote of Umeko's teaching:

> In my class, Miss Tsuda taught translation in the first year, grammar in the second year, and English poetry and composition in the third year. Her Japanese was not a hindrance to daily conversation, but it was not as fluent as her English when the need arose. However, her natural talent and unusual enthusiasm more than compensated for her lack of knowledge of Japanese language and literature. ... Although her major at a US college was biology, she was a gifted language teacher. On more than one occasion, the subtle flavors and shades of the English language, which are hard to name, or the knack or

> the breadth of English writing, were brought home to me by her enthusiastic, energetic, and brilliant explanations. (Yamakawa Kikue 1982b, p. 171)

She also explains:

> She was a pioneer in the field of women's education, who, unusually for a women's educator of her time, never spoke of the Ministry of Education's "wise mother, good wife" principle, but rather, advocated women's vocational education as her flag. She was a teacher with a passion for teaching. She was enthusiastic about teaching, and no matter how bad her mood was when she entered the classroom, she would soon forget all about it, and by the end of the class, she would leave with a melting smile and a joke in English, just like an innocent dojo [little girl]. (1972, pp. 132–133; cf. Kawamoto 2001c)

In the English composition class, the students were not simply asked to learn how to express themselves in English, but to write sentences based on their own careful thinking. Hoshino Ai (1884–1972, graduated in 1906) wrote about the English composition class:

> I learned English composition from Miss Tsuda, who was famous for her strictness, in the third grade. She did not like ambiguity or loose ends, so even in English composition, abstract discussions were not enough; we had to be able to draw a concrete picture. For example, it was during the Russo-Japanese War, and when I discussed the question of how to be of service to the nation during this time, I wrote that it

> was important to save money day by day and that one should not be too extravagant with food. She pointed out that even though Japanese people are not very well nourished, it is not enough just to save money, but to give a concrete example, for example, to stop eating meat and instead eat tofu, which is cheap and nutritious. (1990, pp. 20–21)

Hoshino writes, "Although I received direct instruction from Tsuda-sensei for only a year and a half, the thoroughness of her lessons and her strictness in not allowing even the slightest deception was so deeply ingrained in me that I cannot forget it even to this day" (1950, p. 178).

Yoshikawa Toshikazu called Umeko a fierce-tempered person who mercilessly scolded students who were insubordinate, poorly behaved, or too shy to speak up (1990, p. 269). Whereas Yamakawa respected Umeko's passion as a language teacher, she was critical of her values. Later a socialist and women's activist, Yamakawa had awakened to the disparity between rich and poor before she entered the Eigaku Juku. Yamakawa recounts one episode that occurred in the classroom:

> It was around the time Tolstoy ran away from home, and it came up in class. [Tsuda-] Sensei asked who here had read Tolstoy. I raised my hand honestly. She looked at me gloomily and kept going on and on about Tolstoy for the next hour. Here's what she said: "Tolstoy had given up on religion. His work is nothing but corruption, depravity, ignorance, and immorality. His book is pretty harsh. It's just not right for a lady to have it. His ideas are dangerous and frightening. I'd never let my schoolgirls read his books." And so on. (1982b, p. 174)

Umeko often warned Yamakawa through her sister Matsue, a graduate of the school, that her ideas were not good, but Yamakawa quietly refused, saying that she came to the school to learn English, not to be taught her ideas (1972, p. 138). There was a generation gap in values between the two women, who were about the same age as mother and daughter. Yamakawa was strongly opposed to Umeko's conservatism, which aimed to change the consciousness of Japanese women and improve their social status through education, but was unquestioning of the Emperor's state and class society. For Yamakawa, Umeko was a member of the regime's elite, having been part of Japan's modernization policy since she was a child. The characteristics and the mission of Joshi Eigaku Juku aligned with the values and demands of the Meiji era and its ruling class (Yamakawa Kikue 1982b, p. 174).

In contrast, Umeko's concern for Yamakawa's future is apparent in the following passage:

> Two or three years after graduation, I recall that [Tsuda-] sensei asked me if I would be interested in going to Columbia University to study again. She told me that she would be happy to recommend me for a scholarship for East Asian students at Columbia University if I so desired, that I would only need to help her with some work at the Juku after I returned home, and that I could do any other work I wished, including research and writing, and that I could choose any course of study, not limited to English literature, that I wanted. I declined the courtesy for my own reasons, but I thought the offer was made out of concern for my future and the honor of the school, as I was approaching a socialist group at the time. For Miss Tsuda, the school was everything. It seems that in

> order to save the honor of the school, it was necessary to save those who might tarnish it. (ibid. p. 177)

It seems like a bit of a stretch to see Umeko as trying to get Yamakawa to change course by studying in the US to save the honor of the Juku. It seems, rather, that Umeko had high regard for Yamakawa's academic ability and, without giving up on her, approached her about studying abroad and suggested that she teach at the Juku for her own benefit. As Yoshikawa, who had been a secretary at the school for many years, wrote, "When she found talent in every corner of the students gathered around her, she could not pass by them without a calm demeanor. Her mind was occupied with how to develop the students' talent and how to remove obstacles from them" (1990, p. 270). In any case, despite these differences in thinking, the two women had a close friendship in Kamakura in the last years of Umeko's life, as discussed later.

Kamichika Ichiko (1888–1981, graduated in 1913), who was a year below Yamakawa at school, became a member of the Blue Stockings Society led by Hiratsuka Raicho while still a student at the school. Upon her graduation, Umeko arranged for Kamichika to relocate from Tokyo to Hirosaki, a remote northern region of Honshu Island, to assume a teaching position at the Aomori Prefectural Girls' School. Umeko's hatred of the Blue Stockings Society for disturbing women's morals reveals her conservatism. But her decision not to expel Kamichika from the school was evidence of her care for her student. Later, Kamichika became a newspaper reporter, but her life took an unexpected turn when she fell in love with the charismatic anarchist Osugi Sakae (1885–1923). Unfortunately for her, Osugi had other lovers, leading a jealous Kamichika to stab him in 1916, in what came to be known as the "Hayama Hikage Chaya incident,"[3] for which she was sentenced to two years in prison. After the war, she was elected to the House of Representatives as a member of the Japan Socialist Party, where she worked on women's issues and human rights, such as helping to pass the Anti-Prostitution Law (Kamichika 1972, pp. 397–400).

Days of Farewell

By 1920, a succession of Umeko's close relatives and friends had passed away. Her father Sen suffered a cerebral hemorrhage on the train from Tokyo to his home in Kamakura in April 1908, shortly after Umeko's return from a year-long tour of Europe and the United States. He was 70 years old. Her mother, Hatsuko, passed away in Kamakura in August of the following year. Two months later, Ito Hirobumi, who had looked after Umeko when she returned from her first US study trip (see Ch. 1), was assassinated in Harbin, Manchuria. Umeko's elder sister, Ueno Kotoko (married to Ueno Eizaburo, a businessman), died in May 1911 at the age of 49. Mrs. Lanman, Umeko's American "foster mother" died in February 1914, and Alice Bacon, who had been a volunteer teacher at the Juku since its founding, died in May 1918.

Oyama Sutematsu's husband Iwao passed away in 1916. Sutematsu had devoted herself to the Joshi Eigaku Juku, serving as an advisor and board member, as well as president

---

3 The incident was named after the tea house, Hikage Chaya, in Hayama, Kanagawa Prefecture, where the incident occurred.

of the alumni association. Umeko had been convalescing from diabetes and asthma since the spring of 1917, and in January 1919, formally tendered her resignation to the school council. Sutematsu, Nitobe Inazo, and others decided to nominate Tsuji (née Okonogi) Matsu (1882–1965), the school's lecturer, as Acting Principal. Tsuji had graduated from the Women's Higher Normal School with a major in literature. After studying in the US and England, she served as a professor at her alma mater, but resigned upon her marriage, and had subsequently been a lecturer at the Joshi Eigaku Juku.[4]

A global influenza pandemic, known as the "Spanish flu," had plagued Japan since the previous Autumn. There were three major outbreaks in Japan from August 1918 to March 1921, infecting 23.8 million people, or about 40% of the population of 55 million at the time, and killing nearly 390,000 people. Of these, the first wave had the greatest number of infections and deaths (Naimu-sho Eisei-kyoku (ed.) 2008). Especially in large cities like Tokyo, the numbers infected increased rapidly, and from late October 1918, Eigaku Juku prohibited boarding school students from going out.

Fearing that her grandchildren might be infected, Sutematsu retreated with her family to her villa in Numazu, Kanagawa Prefecture. She would have remained there if not for Umeko's resignation. Sutematsu could not stop thinking about Umeko's successor, so she returned to Tokyo alone. At the Oyama family's house in Tokyo, the houseboys and maids were struck with the Spanish flu in rapid succession, and Sutematsu

4 It appears that it was Nitobe who recommended Tsuji Matsu. In 1933, Tsuji became the first chairperson of Tsuda Eigaku Juku (Tsuda Juku Daigaku 100 nenshi hensan iinkai (ed.) 2003, pp. 120–124).

became infected and developed a fever. Nevertheless, she visited Tsuji's house and persuaded her to become the acting principal despite the latter's hesitation. On February 5, she attended Tsuji's inauguration as acting principal with a sense of relief that she had fulfilled her responsibility. Immediately thereafter, she developed a sore throat and a fever of nearly 40°C. She developed pneumonia and died on February 18 at the age of 58. While fighting her own illnesses, Umeko was held by those around her and attended the funeral of her best friend, whom she loved like a sister (Kuno 1993a, pp. 327–329; Kuno 1993b, pp. 237–239). Later that year, Umeko suffered two cerebral hemorrhages and was repeatedly in and out of St. Luke's Hospital.

Umeko nevertheless lived another 10 years. She had fallen ill just as her school was getting off the ground, and suffered a great deal of inner turmoil before deciding to retire. At first, she was frustrated, feeling worthless if she could not work. Soon, however, the frustration turned to resignation. In a diary entry of June 13, 1917, she wrote:

> I should not linger too long on myself. I must learn how little I and my work count in the eternal scheme of things—that one seed must be crushed and ground down that the new plant may come out. I think the same can be said about me and the school. Is it so with me and the school? That is what is on my mind. (reproduced in Yoshikawa 1990, p. 249)

This passage seems to reflect her faith. It is similar to John 12:24 in the Bible: "Very truly I tell you, unless a kernel of wheat falls to the ground and dies, it remains only a single seed. But if it dies, it produces many seeds." However, Kawamoto

Figure 4.8 Umeko in her later years, 1927. Courtesy Tsuda University Archives.

Shizuko, a scholar of English literature and Umeko, reads the passage as reflective of Umeko's knowledge of biology and the natural world:

> [In this passage], one can sense a calm and sober look at the affairs of the natural world. She may have been a young woman who majored in biology at Bryn Mawr College in the US, and the scientific eye she cultivated through her biology may have made her quietly accept the natural world, where seedlings sprout and seeds die, even in the midst of similar circumstances. (2001a, pp. 14–15; cf. Sueki 2001)

In her later years, Umeko, who was known for her sharp temper, became so calm that her appearance changed.

Although her home was in Goten-yama, Kita-shinagawa in Tokyo, Umeko spent the summers in a small villa she had built on a mountainside in Inamuragasaki, Kamakura. The villa was destroyed in the Great Kanto Earthquake of September 1, 1923, and for a while after that, she used Nitobe Inazo's nearby villa as her summer house. In November 1928, another dear friend, Uryu Shigeko, died of colon cancer at the age of 67. In the spring of the following year, 1929, she rebuilt her villa in Inamuragasaki and moved there in July. Reading and knitting became her modest daily routine. Graduates sometimes visited her. She spent a quiet summer sitting on a chair on the porch facing the ocean at Shichirigahama (Seven-mile Beach), listening to the sound of the waves and enjoying the sea breeze. It might have reminded her of her summer at Woods Hole. On August 16, she died of a cerebral hemorrhage after 64 years of life.[5]

Yamakawa Kikue, a former student of Umeko's, had moved to Inamuragasaki with her husband Hitoshi (1880–1958), a socialist thinker, three years earlier to care for their sickly child and were thus close neighbors in Umeko's final days (see the chronological table in Yamakawa Kikue 1982a). When Kikue delivered homegrown vegetables and flowers, Umeko apparently was "delighted like a child" (1982b, p. 176; Tsuda Michio 2012, pp. 38–39). Umeko once visited Yamakawa's house with help, it was too far for her to manage on her own. When Umeko passed away, Yamakawa was present. In an obituary she wrote for a magazine, she described Umeko as

5 Umeko first built a villa in Inamuragasaki, Kamakura, around 1907. After Umeko's death, people associated with the school used it. Yamada Koto, a professor at the Joshi Eigaku Juku, was a caretaker of the villa. She first met the renowned philosopher Nishida Kitaro (1870–1945) here and later married him (Tsuda Michio 2012, pp. 37–39; Yoshikawa 1990, p. 250; Ueda Hisashi 1986, pp. 46–64).

"a strong woman who devoted her life completely to her work and bravely and without regret chose a life of solitude because of the mission she was given" (1982b, pp. 177–178).

Chapter 5

From Juku to Daigaku

Given Ms. Tsuda Umeko's initial major in biology and her interest in the natural sciences, as well as her guidance of her students in their daily observations of nature, it is evident that the establishment of the new department [of science] is not in conflict with her will or with the existing administrative policy of the school.

– Report of the Deliberative Committee on the Future Administration Policy of Tsuda Eigaku Juku, 1942

It is with great pleasure that we confront this decisive battle with the glorious hope of establishing an exceptional and distinctive science department within the robust academic culture [of Tsuda Juku]. This initiative will pave the way for numerous young women, endowed with talent in this domain, to access higher education and address the needs of the nation by enhancing the status of Japanese women.

– Hoshino Ai,
"On the Establishment of the New Department," 1943

With the strengthening of domestic conditions, the importance of education for girls has increased by another hundred steps. It is essential for female scientists to become science teachers at girls' schools, junior high schools, and normal schools, as well as researchers and assistants at various scientific research institutes.

– Fujita Taki,
"Recent Situation of the Science Department," 1943

Many trees that grew from the "one seed" named Tsuda Umeko eventually bore diverse flowers and fruits (Kawamoto et al. 2001; Mamtkulova 2011b; Tsuda Juku Daigaku soritsu 100 shunen kinen-shi shuppan iinkai (ed.) 2000). Among them, Hoshino Ai, who was 20 years younger than Umeko, was the disciple whom Umeko entrusted with the future of the school. During World War II, when English education was in danger of extinction, Hoshino kept the school alive by founding the science department, and after the war, she served as the first president of the new Tsuda College. This chapter explores what the young Hoshino saw and learned from her study at Bryn Mawr College, Umeko's alma mater. It then examines how that experience influenced her later education and management at the school, leading to the founding of the new postwar college.[1]

Hoshino Ai and Her Study at Bryn Mawr

Hoshino Ai was born in Gunma Prefecture in the Kanto region of Honshu. After completing eight years of the common and advanced grades at Numata Elementary School, she studied for five years at Ferris Waei Girls' School, a mission school founded in 1870 in Yokohama, where her elder brother was a teacher. She was baptized at the age of 12. At Ferris Waei, there was Bible class every day. When she reached the advanced level, she took Bible classes in English. Eager to continue her studies, she took the entrance examination for

1 On Hoshino's life and career, see Kawamoto 2001b; Ueda 2000; Tsuda Juku Rika no rekishi wo kiroku suru kai (ed.) 1987, pp. 147–163; Ueno et al. 2000; and Koizumi 2008.

Joshi Eigaku Juku on the recommendation of a senior student at Ferris. Hoshino's autobiography describes what happened in the summer of 1904 when she visited Joshi Eigaku Juku to inquire about the entrance examination:

> At that time, a clerk by the very old-fashioned name of Ms. Godai-in was taking care of all the general affairs of the school. Ms. Godai-in's reply was that the entrance examination consisted of English, Japanese, Chinese classics, and mathematics, and either botany or zoology as biology. I thought I would be fine in English since I had been trained at Ferris, but I was not confident at all in mathematics and biology, so I concentrated on studying these two subjects during the summer vacation.
>
> However, when I took the entrance examination in September, I found that there were only three tests: English, Japanese, and Chinese Classics. The Japanese and Chinese writing were easy, but the English examination was made very meticulously. (1990, p. 19)

It is unclear why the administrative staff made a mistake in the subjects of the entrance examination. Thanks to that mistake, however, Hoshino studied mathematics and biology intensively for a short period, which influenced her later choices in life.

After passing the examination, Hoshino was accepted into second year on the condition that she take first-year grammar and history. She learned history in English from Kawai Michi (1877–1953), who had just returned from the United States. Kawai had studied at Bryn Mawr College under the American Women's Scholarship for Japanese Women program, which

Umeko had established with donations from the US. Upon her return to Japan, Kawai became a teacher at Joshi Eigaku Juku. According to Hoshino, "Kawai-sensei was wonderfully dressed in Western-style clothing at the time, and her dashing appearance and enthusiastic teaching style made her a popular figure among the students" (1990, p. 20). Kawai was well respected by people around her, as evidenced by the fact that when she established Keisen Girls' School in 1929, Joshi Eigaku Juku's students organized a maintenance group called the "Small Flock of Disciples (*chiisaki deshi no mure*)" to raise funds and support her school (see Kimura 2002, Chapter IV).

Upon graduating from Joshi Eigaku Juku in 1906, Hoshino was employed as a teacher at Shizuoka Eiwa School, where she taught English and sometimes mathematics. After one semester, Umeko encouraged her to study at Bryn Mawr College on the American Women's Scholarship for Japanese Women, starting in September, which is indicative of Umeko's high regard for Hoshino. The first recipient of this scholarship was Matsuda Michi from Ferris (who studied at Bryn Mawr College in 1893–1899, and later became president of Doshisha Women's School). The second was Kawai Michi (who studied at Bryn Mawr in 1898–1994, and later founded Keisen Girls' School), and the third was Suzuki Utako (who studied at Bryn Mawr in 1904–1906, and later became professor at Women's Gakushuin). Hoshino was the fourth (Uchida 2000). To pass the entrance examination for Bryn Mawr College, Hoshino spent two years at a preparatory school in the US, carefully preparing for the entrance examination in English, mathematics, history, science, and other subjects.

During the entrance examination, she drew the attention of Charlotte Angas Scott (1858–1931), a professor of mathematics, because of the unique way she had solved a geometry problem in mathematics. Scott was a female mathematician from England and the first chair of the Department of Mathematics at Bryn Mawr. She believed that Hoshino had a talent for mathematics and encouraged her to pursue studies in mathematics after enrolling at the school. Although Hoshino was not too keen on the idea, she took trigonometry and equation theory in her first year and matrix geometry in her second year. However, she eventually decided that she could not keep up with them and stopped taking math-related courses. She refers to this incident as "a tragicomedy caused by the entrance examination" (1990, p. 33; cf. Hoshino, Transcript, 1908–1912, Bryn Mawr College Special Collections).

In October 1908, she entered the university. The president of Bryn Mawr College at the time was M. Carey Thomas, who had been the dean when Umeko was there. Hoshino writes of Thomas:

> She was not the family type. She believed that women did not need to learn how to cook, sew, and so on, as long as they were passionate about their studies and research. She also believed that men and women should be equal. I believe such views of the president were reflected in the fact that Bryn Mawr students were said to be "highbrow" or scary. (1990, p. 41)

Bryn Mawr required undergraduates to choose two majors after completing the two-year liberal arts program. Although she was encouraged to major in English literature, Hoshino chose biology and chemistry. As she recalls:

> I did not necessarily follow Tsuda-sensei's advice. But I chose biology and chemistry, as I was afraid of too much reading. Therefore, for the next two years, the library was replaced by the laboratory as the center of my studies. I started by dissecting worms, and eventually went on to dissect rabbits and sheep, which I consider to have been another valuable learning experience. Besides my major subjects, I chose English literature for all my electives. (1990, p. 43)

Despite her claims that she chose biology and chemistry out of fear of extensive reading, it is more likely to have been a proactive decision, considering Hoshino's prior experience with science-related studies. According to Hoshino's transcript (stored at the Bryn Mawr College Special Collections), she took a minor in physics in her second year, a minor in chemistry and a major in biology in her third year, and a major in chemistry in her fourth year. All of these were full-year courses that combined lectures (first semester) and laboratory work (second semester) (see Chapter 2 for course-work details). Outside of the sciences she took History of English Literature, Composition, and Elocution (first and second year), German (third year), Philosophy, Psychology, and Reading Shakespeare (fourth year) (Hoshino, Transcript 1908–1912, Bryn Mawr College Special Collections).

The faculty of the Biology Department at Bryn Mawr had changed significantly from that of twenty years earlier when Umeko was there (Bryn Mawr College, 1912, pp. 173–179). Only Warren remained from Umeko's time, as an assistant

Figure 5.1 Bryn Mawr College, graduating class of 1912. Hoshino Ai is second from right in the back row. Courtesy Bryn Mawr College Special Collections.

professor of physiology. The central figure in the department in Hoshino's time was Professor David Hilt Tennent (1873–1941). Hoshino took his major course in biology in her junior year. Tennent had been a student of William Brooks at Johns Hopkins University. He later visited Japan twice to conduct fieldwork at the Misaki Marine Biological Station of Tokyo Imperial University. The Great Kanto Earthquake occurred during his first visit to Japan in the summer of 1923, resulting in the loss of his notebooks and specimens (Gardiner 1951).[2]

Harriet Randolph, who taught botany, and Nettie Maria Stevens (1861–1912), a geneticist known for her work on chromosome sex determination (she discovered the Y chromosome), were also faculty members in the department.

2 Hoshino recalled, "One of my unforgettable memories in connection with my old studies is that of my biology teacher, Dr. Tennant, who visited Japan later in life, and was deeply saddened by the loss of all the rare fish and shellfish he had collected from the seas around Japan in the Great Kanto Earthquake" (1990, p. 43).

Stevens died of breast cancer shortly before Hoshino's graduation (Brush 1978).

As a special student at Bryn Mawr, Umeko was not obliged to choose two majors, as Hoshino did as an undergraduate student. Umeko could thus take many specialized courses in biology. Hoshino mostly took major courses and graduated without any specialized post-major courses. Umeko's embryological study of frogs with Morgan was done in a post-major course. Umeko also attended an intensive summer course at Woods Hole and worked as a laboratory assistant at Bryn Mawr. Whereas Umeko had received a highly specialized biology education, Hoshino was not trained as a researcher. Nevertheless, Hoshino's study at Bryn Mawr was something of a "reliving" of Umeko's journey, as she experienced the conditions of women's science education in the US, which was invaluable when she later established the science department at Eigaku Juku.

Hoshino returned to Japan in the summer of 1912 with a Bachelor of Arts degree and began teaching at Joshi Eigaku Juku in September. She wrote in her autobiography that she taught English language and literature, as well as biology:

> Somehow my teaching career got back on track, but I was very annoyed when Tsuda-sensei asked me to teach this and that, partly because she was short of teachers. She even asked me to teach the Bible, British history, and the history of linguistics, which I had not studied in the United States. She said that I could teach physiology because I majored in biology. Although I refused to teach physiology, I taught biology in the preparatory or special departments of the time. (1990, p. 56)

She then recounts an episode:

> In the middle of the biology class, Nitobe-sensei suddenly walked in. Taking this advantage, I asked him to teach something. He immediately drew a picture of a skull on the blackboard and explained the difference between the skulls of white and colored races. I was so impressed by his erudition. (ibid., pp. 56–57)

Nitobe Inazo was originally an agricultural researcher with a deep knowledge of biology and population studies.

In the 1910s, "biology" was not offered as a regular course of study at Joshi Eigaku Juku, so it appears that Hoshino substituted biology for "physiology" in the practical training program called "home economics," which was established at Umeko's request (Tsuda Umeko 1895). The Department of Home Economics was established in April 1909 and approved as a so-called "separate department" under the Vocational School Ordinance. Kawashima Yoshiko (born in 1875), one of the first graduates of Joshi Eigaku Juku, who had studied chemistry and home economics at Simmons College in Boston, was the first head of the department. It was a two-year course of study, with English as the main subject. Other subjects offered included bookkeeping, hygiene, physiology, and cooking. It was renamed the Department of Practical Training (*Jisshu-ka*) in 1912. However, due to low enrollment, it was discontinued in 1919 (Tsuda Juku Daigaku 100 nenshi hensan iinkai (ed.) 2003, pp. 85–86).

As discussed in Chapter 4, Umeko fell ill in May 1917. The following year, perhaps considering her successor, she encouraged Hoshino to return to the US for further studies.

Figure 5.2 Joshi Eigaku Juku, October 3, 1924, when Umeko visited from her sickbed. One year after the Great Kanto Earthquake, in front of the Gobancho temporary school building. Front row, from right: Yamada Koto (later Mrs. Nishida Kitaro), Kanie Misao, Hoshino Ai, Tsuda Umeko, Tsuji Matsu (acting principal). Back row, from right: Yoshikawa Toshikazu, Nakagiri Kakutaro (pedagogy and ethics), fourth person is Kasuya Yoshi (later the second president of Tsuda College), and seventh person is Ruth Ray Tamson. Courtesy Tsuda University Archives.

Figure 5.3 Hoshino Ai at the time of her appointment as acting principal. Courtesy Tsuda University Archives.

She attended the Teachers College of Columbia University in New York for a year, received a Master of Arts degree in education, and returned to Japan in September 1919.

Figure 5.4 The new school building in Kodaira, shortly after completion. In 1931, the school moved from Gobancho to Kodaira, and changed its name to Tsuda Eigaku Juku in 1933. Courtesy Tsuda University Archives.

Upon returning to Japan, Hoshino had a busy and difficult road ahead of her. She served as vice principal under acting principal Tsuji, became acting principal in 1925, and became the second principal after Umeko's death in 1929. In 1931, the school campus relocated to Kodaira. Two years later, the school became a foundation, changing its name to Tsuda Eigaku Juku. During the Pacific War (1941–1945), Hoshino played a pivotal role in establishing a science department. After the war, the juku underwent a transformation into Tsuda College, and she was appointed as its inaugural president. The next section will discuss Hoshino's path to establishing the science department.

Creating the Science Department during the War

The movement to elevate women's vocational schools to universities, which had been proposed several times, was never realized due to opposition to women's education, as discussed in Chapter 4. Thus, higher education for women before the war was limited to the government-run women's higher normal schools and private vocational schools. In this context, the number of women's vocational schools steadily increased. Eight women's vocational schools, including Joshi Eigaku Jyuku, had been approved during the Meiji era (1868–1912),[3] but during the Taisho period (1912–1926) there was a rush to establish new schools, resulting in 16 new schools.[4] One problem with women's vocational schools was that, although graduates were awarded secondary education diplomas and qualified to teach, they were concentrated in fields such as Japanese literature, English literature, and home economics. Training women to teach in mathematics, physics, chemistry, biology, and other science subjects was the exclusive domain of the Women's Higher Normal Schools (one in Tokyo and one

---

3 The rest are: Japan Women's University, Aoyama Women's School (English Department), Imperial Women's Vocational School, Kobe College Vocational School, Tokyo Women's Theological Vocational School, Doshisha Women's School (Senmon-bu), and Tokyo Women's Medical Vocational School.

4 These are: Sacred Heart Women's Higher Vocational School, Tokyo Woman's Christian University, Kassui Women's Vocational School, Kyoto Women's Vocational School, Toyo Women's Vocational School of Dental Medicine, Tokyo Women's Vocational School, Baika Women's Vocational School, Fukuoka Prefectural Women's Vocational School, Japan Women's Vocational School of Dental Medicine, Osaka Prefectural Women's Vocational School, Imperial Women's Vocational School of Pharmacy, Jissen Women's Vocational School, Imperial Women's Medical Vocational School, Kyoritsu Women's Vocational School, Shoin Women's Vocational School, and Miyagi Prefectural Women's Vocational School (Hatanaka 2004, p. 216).

in Nara) (Murata 1980, p. 52). The only vocational schools that offered women education in science and mathematics were Japan Women's University (School of Home Economics and of Education) and Tokyo Woman's Christian University (Department of Mathematics). Neither school was recognized as a university under the University Ordinance (*Daigaku Rei*, promulgated in 1918) despite their names, but they were instead defined as vocational schools under the Vocational School Ordinance (promulgated in 1903).

Nukada Yutaka (1878–1972), the founder of the Imperial Women's Medical and Pharmaceutical Vocational School (Teikoku Joshi Igaku Yakugaku Senmon Gakko, a private vocational school), had long considered the "cultivation and development of natural scientific knowledge" among Japanese women to be of vital importance. He had the idea of founding a women's science school that would be as good as the Women's Higher Normal School, and repeatedly appealed to the Ministry of Education for its creation. However, according to Nukada, the bureaucrats at the Ministry of Education refused to listen, saying, "There is no way girls can have a scientific mind," "If we let girls study science, they will lose their femininity," and "There will probably be no applicants" (Kato Kyosuke 1955, p. 125; Nukada 1942).

With the outbreak of the Pacific War, however, the Ministry of Education's negative attitude toward scientific education for women changed dramatically. As increasing numbers of men went off to war, there was a serious shortage of secondary school science teachers and scientists, and science education was instantly promoted at women's vocational schools. In October 1943, the Cabinet approved the "Emergency Wartime Measures Concerning Education," and women's vocational schools suddenly began offering new science majors across Japan.[5]

In fact, the Ministry of Education's policy had changed several years before the Cabinet officially issued the emergency measures. The Imperial Women's Vocational School of Science (Teikoku Joshi Rigaku Senmon Gakko), which Nukada had long advocated for, was approved and opened in 1941, becoming Japan's first independent science school for women, consisting of departments of mathematics, physics, chemistry, and biology (Toho Daigaku Rigakubu 50 shunen kinen jigyo iinkai (ed.) 1991).

---

5 Four schools had been approved to teach science to women by the end of 1943, including Teikoku Women's Vocational School of Science (newly established), Kyoto Prefectural Women's Vocational School, Women's Vocational School of Economics, and Tsuda Juku Vocational School. In 1944, approval was granted to: Tokyo Prefectural Women's Vocational School, Osaka Prefectural Women's Vocational School, Miyagi Prefectural Women's Vocational School, Hiroshima Prefectural Women's Vocational School, Fukuoka Prefectural Women's Vocational School, Shoin Women's Vocational School, Otani Women's Vocational School (newly established), Koka Women's Vocational School (newly established), Okayama Seishin Women's Vocational School (newly established), Kochi Prefectural Women's Vocational School, and Suzumine Women's Vocational School.

The School of Home Economics at Japan Women's University had provided science education from its inception in 1901, and in 1944, the Department of Home Economics and Science (Kasei Rika, consisting of the program of physics and chemistry and the program of biology and agricultural science) was added to the School of Home Economics (Tsuda Juku Rika no rekishi wo kiroku suru kai (ed.) 1987, pp. 28, 36–41).

The wartime emergency measures stipulated: "Science and technological universities and vocational schools shall be expanded and improved, and liberal arts universities and vocational schools shall be converted to science schools," and "Women's vocational schools shall be revised as necessary so that their educational content can provide vocational education that is a better alternative to men's workplace" (National Diet Library Research 1943).

Tsuda Eigaku Juku's creation of a science department was certainly part of this trend, but circumstances had already demanded that the school add new departments. As the Pacific War was about to break out, the school had to confront some difficulties. Hoshino Ai, the principal of the school, recalled the following after the war:

> [The difficulties were] the shortsighted attitude of the authorities toward foreign languages, especially English education, and the general public's indifference to the same. From its inception, Tsuda was a school specializing mainly in English language and literature, and everyone at Tsuda was determined that no other school would be able to match it in this area. However, relations with Britain, the US, and other English-speaking countries continued to deteriorate, and by the time the war broke out, many schools with English literature departments were forced to switch to other departments. The general public also accepted this policy and became fearful and reserved about allowing their children to study English. Although the Ministry of Education did not demand that Tsuda abolish the English Department, students could not help but feel the pressure of society from all angles. One time, a student rushed into the principal's office and tearfully complained that she was reading an English book on the train on her way to school when a man came in front of her and snatched the book from her, cursing her in front of everyone that Japan could not win the war because there were people who read such things. (Hoshino 1955, pp. 177–178)

English was considered an enemy language. English had already been removed as a required subject from all girls' high schools in Japan, becoming an optional subject, and was even on its way to being abolished. Under these circumstances, the number of English teachers was drastically decreasing, and the number of students at Tsuda Eigaku Juku was also decreasing year by year. Hoshino felt that she had no choice but to visit Hashida Kunihiko (1882–1945), a physician and physiologist who had become Minister of Education in 1940, and appeal to him that English education was necessary no matter how fierce the war became (Hoshino 1990, p. 92). Nevertheless, nothing could be done about the sharp decline in the number of students taking the entrance examinations and the resulting decrease in the number of students enrolling.

Hoshino recalls, "I originally thought that a school that taught only English was unsound. I had long hoped to develop it into a school with various other departments" (1990, p. 93). As mentioned in the previous section, a department of home economics was established, later becoming a practical training department, but it was abolished due to low enrollment. Additionally, a department of commerce, a department of philosophy (humanities), and a department of Japanese literature had been considered, but never realized.

In the summer of 1942, Hoshino organized a deliberative committee consisting of 15 members, including directors, councilors (including Inoue Jinkichi, an applied chemist, former president of Tohoku Imperial University and president of the Society of Industrial Chemistry), alumni association officers, and people related to the school, to discuss the future development of the school. The committee investigated the majors of women's vocational schools in Japan. As a result, according to Hoshino, "What is currently lacking most among Japanese women is education in the sciences, and therefore

Tsuda concluded that the most desirable thing to do at this time was to add a small but solid science department at all costs" (1955, p. 178). Establishing a science department could bring the school back from the brink of disaster.

The committee submitted its report to the Board of Directors in September 1942. It proposed establishing four "sub-departments" within the Science Department: "The Science Department [Rika] shall include the sub-departments of mathematics, biology, physics and chemistry, geology and mineralogy" and others. The report explained the reason for the expansion as follows: "Given Ms. Tsuda Umeko's initial major in biology and her interest in the natural sciences, as well as her guidance of her students in their daily observations of nature, it is evident that the establishment of the new department is not in conflict with her will or with the existing administrative policy of the school" (quoted in Hoshino 1943, p. 3). Clearly, Hoshino was determined to break through the socially accepted notion that "science is a man's study," and to take this opportunity to open a path to science for women. The report also stated, "In accordance with the will of the authorities of the Ministry of Education, it is their policy to permit the establishment of various science departments under the prevailing circumstances" (ibid., p. 4).

After receiving the report, deliberations at an extraordinary meeting of the Board of Directors, and final consideration within the school, it was decided that the science department would be reduced to two sub-departments: Mathematics, and Physics and Chemistry. There is no documentary evidence to indicate why the other two sub-departments were excluded at this stage, but there were problems with facilities, funding, and personnel. However, courses in biology (first year), physiology (first year), and geology and mineralogy (second year) were included in the curriculum of the Department of Physics and Chemistry (Tsuda Juku Rika no rekishi wo kiroku suru kai (ed.) 1987, p. 77).

Unlike the Imperial Women's Vocational School of Science, which had medical and pharmaceutical teaching facilities and faculty at affiliated schools before its establishment, establishing a science department at an English-language school was a laborious process. The school received detailed advice on science classrooms, chemistry laboratories, and other facilities from Professor Emeritus Matsubara Koichi (1871–1955) of Tokyo Imperial University, who had enrolled his daughter at Tsuda Eigaku Juku, and his student Takehara Kumakichi (1883–1957), a professor at the Higher Normal School. Hoshino recalls, "Unlike the liberal arts department, it was a great challenge to set up the facilities. There were no gas facilities deep in the forests of Musashino, of course. We even had to purchase a gas generator" (1990, p. 98). During the war, purchasing microscopes, balances, and other necessary machinery and equipment required complicated procedures of approval and procurement. The Ministry of Education did not grant approval for the new department until the necessary equipment was obtained. The project was funded by donations from the alumni association. On Matsubara's recommendation, Kuwaki Ayao (1878–1945), a professor emeritus at Kyushu Imperial University, was appointed head of the science department. Once the science department was established, the school changed its name from Tsuda Eigaku Juku to Tsuda Juku Senmon Gakko (Tsuda Juku Vocational School), dropping the word "Eigaku (English studies)" from the name, although the Department of English was retained (it was renamed the Department of Foreign Languages in March 1944).

The science department was approved in January 1943. In the alumni bulletin that February, Hoshino reported:

> It is with great pleasure that we confront this decisive battle with the glorious hope of establishing an exceptional and distinctive science department within the robust academic culture [of Tsuda Juku]. This initiative will pave the way for numerous young women, endowed with talent in this domain, to access higher education and address the needs of the nation by enhancing the status of Japanese women. (1943, p. 7)

In April 1943, the science department welcomed new students and began classes in a new four-year course of study. There were 62 applicants for the first year in the Department of Mathematics and 99 for the Department of Physics and Chemistry. After an entrance examination (in mathematics and Japanese, but not English), 26 students were admitted to the Department of Mathematics and 32 to the Department of Physics and Chemistry (Tsuda Juku Daigaku 100 nenshi hensan iinkai 2003, vol. 1, p. 203). The new students included a woman in her forties who was a mathematics teacher at a girls' school, a woman who had worked for many years in the astrophysics department of Kyoto Imperial University, and students from as far away as Harbin, Dalian, and Taiwan (Fujita 1943, pp. 8–9). Fujita Taki (1898–1993, later the third president of Tsuda College), who was in charge of the science class, wrote an article in the alumni bulletin in December that year titled "Recent Situation of the Science Department," in which she stated:

> With the strengthening of domestic conditions, the importance of education for girls has increased by another hundred steps. It is essential for female scientists to become science teachers at girls' schools, junior high schools, and normal schools, as well as researchers and assistants at various scientific research institutes… The responsibility of the Tsuda Science Department is heavy and great. (ibid., p. 12)[6]

When the science department opened, the courses offered included: Mathematical Analysis (Kuroda Takao, professor at Tokyo Academy of Physics), Algebra (Ooi Koshiro, lecturer at the Second Faculty of Engineering, Tokyo Imperial University), Geometric Triads (Ogawa Junjiro, professor at the Army Aviation Technical School), Analytical Geometry (Yamazaki Saburo, professor at Seijo High School), Introduction to Chemistry (Takehara Kumakichi, professor at the Tokyo Higher Normal School), Introduction to Physics (Mitsuishi Iwao), and Biology and Physiology (Furukawa Haruo, professor at Nihon University). Of these, only Mitsuishi Iwao (1901–1997) was a full-time professor in the Department of Physics and Chemistry; the rest were adjunct lecturers with other schools. Mitsuishi was employed at Tsuda College on the recommendation of Sugai Junichi (1903–1982), a physics graduate of Tokyo Imperial University and a science official at the Ministry of Education. As a bureaucrat, Sugai is believed to have assisted in establishing the science department. Takehara Kumakichi, then president of the

6 Fujita Taki graduated from Joshi Eigaku Juku in 1920, studied at Bryn Mawr College (majoring in history and economics) from 1921 to 1925, and taught at her alma mater after returning to Japan (Fujita 1971; Fujita Taki-sensei no ronshu to omoide sewanin-kai (ed.) 1993).

Chemical Society of Japan, was recommended by Matsubara Koichi to teach chemistry classes. Hayashi Taro (1903–1988), a professor at Tokyo Women's Higher Normal School, was also a part-time lecturer in chemistry from 1944. Okajima Masae (1912–1987), a female graduate of Tokyo Bunrika University, later became a full-time professor of chemistry (Tsuda Juku Rika no rekishi wo kiroku suru kai (ed.) 1987, pp. 63–64; Tsuda Juku Daigaku soritsu 100 shunen kinen-shi shuppan iinkai (ed.) 2003, vol. 1, pp. 198–199).

Although English was not on the entrance examination, Fujita Taki, the homeroom teacher, required five hours of English classes per week for first-year students, saying, "When we open science at Tsuda, it is natural that we want to produce scientists who can read original books without hesitation" (Fujita 1943, p. 11). The curriculum was similar to that of the Tokyo Academy of Physics (Tokyo Butsuri Gakko, approved as a vocational school in 1917, later became Tokyo University of Science), and the school policy was to provide high-quality education without any disparity between male and female students (Tsuda Juku Rika no rekishi wo kiroku suru kai (ed.) 1987, p. 75; Tanioka 1998, p. 505).

Kuwaki Ayao, head of the entire science department, had been a professor at the Faculty of Engineering of Kyushu Imperial University and then the principal of Matsumoto High School before arriving at Tsuda Juku. He was a physicist as well as a historian and philosopher of science. Kuwaki was a longtime friend of Albert Einstein (1879–1955) and had introduced the theory of relativity to Japan. He did not teach classes, but instead, until his sudden death in May 1945, devoted himself to establishing the foundation of the science department. Kuroda (1913–91), a professor at Tokyo

Figure 5.5 Kuwaki Ayao with Albert Einstein and his wife at Kyushu Imperial University, December 1922. Kuwaki (second from left in the front row) did not teach classes in the science department, but would sometimes talk to students about Einstein during extracurricular activities. Courtesy Kyushu University Archives.

Academy of Physics, was put in charge of mathematics at Kuwaki's invitation (Yajima 1949; Ito 2015, 2016).

The people involved in science in that pioneering lineup includes many who were interested in the history of science and associated with the History of Science Society of Japan, which was founded in April 1941 on the initiative of Sugai and others. Kuwaki was the society's first president, Sugai the managing advisor, Matsubara Koichi an advisor, and Furukawa Haruo was secretary (Doke 1996; Okada 2009). Kuwaki contributed "Research on the History of Science" and Furukawa "Addendum to 'Siebold Studies'" to the first issue of the society's organ, *Kagakusi Kenkyu* (Study of the History of Science), published in December 1941. Kuroda was a mathematician as well as a historian of mathematics and served as the society's seventh president after the war.

Mitsuishi also had a deep knowledge and authored numerous books on the history of science and biographies of scientists. As these personal connections influenced the Tsuda Juku faculty, it is unsurprising that their classes often covered topics in the history of science.

While education was beginning, the war situation was deteriorating. In 1944, the school year was shortened to three years, and students were mobilized to work at the Hitachi Aircraft factory on campus, making parts for fighter planes. More than one hundred first- and second-year science students were assigned to work on calculations on the propagation of radio waves, a research project for the Ministry of Education's Radio Physics Research Institute (Dempa Butsuri Kenkyusho) (Tsuda Juku Rika no rekishi wo kiroku suru kai (ed.) 1987, pp. 84–88). In between these assignments, the students continued their school studies. The war ended on August 15, 1945. The faculty, staff, and students all gathered in the dormitory cafeteria to hear the war's final edict on the radio, after which, Hoshino's first words to the stunned students were, "Come on, everyone, let's study. Let's make up for what we have not been able to do until now" (ibid., p. 160).

In the chaos immediately following the war, it was a full year before classes began to get back on track. In 1948, after its fifth cohort of science students enrolled, the school was reestablished as Tsuda College (Tsuda Juku Daigaku) under the new education system, and the science department closed its doors.

Figure 5.6 Students working in a munitions factory on campus. In 1944, the school opened a plant on the Kodaira campus. The school offered its facilities, including the gymnasium and student rooms, for factory work. This provided students with a safer environment than working in an off-campus factory and allowed them time for classes. Courtesy Tsuda University Archives.

Figure 5.7 Hoshino Ai (front row, center) and first-year science students at graduation in 1947. Despite continuing food shortages, the expressions on people's faces show their relief at the return of a peaceful daily life. In the front row, next to far left is Sato Kimiko. Fifth from the right in the back row is Kasuya Yoshi. Courtesy Tsuda University Archives.

Figure 5.8 Laboratory work in the science department of Tsuda Juku shortly after the war. Photo from "The Science Department 2nd Graduation Album" (1948). Courtesy Tsuda University Archives.

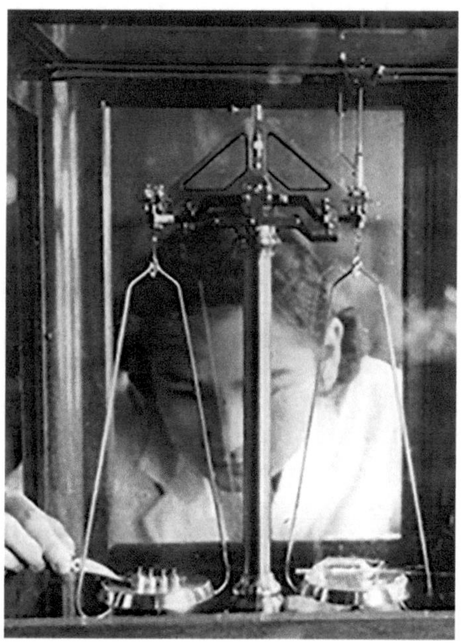

Figure 5.9 A science student using a balance-scale for weighing, shortly after the war. Courtesy Tsuda University Archives.

Toward a "True Daigaku"

In 1946, the United States Education Mission to Japan – a group of 27 education experts from the United States – spent one month in Japan to assess the rebuilding of the education system. They visited schools and conducted various surveys. In response, the Japanese organized a committee of 29 members headed by Nanbara Shigeru (1889–1974), president of Tokyo Imperial University. Hoshino was one of the two women on the committee. The other was Kawai Michi. At a meeting with the US delegation, Hoshino expressed her view that "girls' education had been neglected in Japan, and the Ministry of Education had no understanding of girls' education and was cold toward the development of private schools" (Hoshino 1990, pp. 103–104). The delegation's report to the Supreme Commander of the Allied Powers proposed that more universities should be established and recommended that "girls who are now ready must now be given the freedom to go on to higher education immediately" (United States Education Mission 1946, p. 61).

In February 1947, public and private women's vocational schools and women's higher normal schools formed the Women's University League (Joshi Daigaku Renmei) and united to promote university for women. Lulu Holmes (1899–1977), an advisor to the Civil Information and Educational Section of the General Headquarters of the Allied Forces in Japan, supported this movement. Holmes had studied at Columbia University's graduate school, like Hoshino, and had taught history at Kobe College for one year (1934), so she had personal experience of women's education in Japan. She was determined to have a women's university established while she was in Japan (Hoshino 1990, p. 106; See also Uemura 2007;

Ishii 2000; Kusano and Sewell 1993). Holmes' strong support was sufficient to overcome the resistance within the Ministry of Education, and in March 1948, Tsuda College, Japan Women's University, Tokyo Woman's Christian University, University of the Sacred Heart, and Kobe College were approved for accreditation as four-year universities ahead of other women's universities. Tsuda Umeko's dream of a "true daigaku" was finally realized after half a century. Hoshino recalls, "We may have been a little pushy, but considering the cold shoulder we had received from the Ministry of Education over the years, we were anxious to establish the university, lest we miss the opportunity and suffer the same fate" (1990, p. 106).

The initial proposal by the Tsuda Juku board of directors was to create a women's college with two faculties and five departments: literature (English literature, Japanese literature, and history) and science (mathematics and chemistry). After a review by visiting members of the committee and Ministry of Education officials, the proposed Department of English was almost unanimously supported. By contrast, they were of the opinion that the Department of Mathematics left "room for consideration," while the Department of Chemistry was "inadequate" (Hoshino 1990, p. 105).[7] It appears that the facilities and other aspects of the department were inadequate because the department had been established during the war, when supplies were scarce.

7 The university's board of directors decided against a proposal to establish a physics department due to the difficulties in providing adequate facilities (Tsuda Juku Rika no rekishi wo kiroku suru kai (ed.) 1987, p. 113).

Thus, the English Department's promotion to university status was approved in 1948. In 1949, the Department of Mathematics was approved. Now, Tsuda College had two departments that made up a faculty. The application for the faculty's name was initially submitted as the Faculty of Arts and Sciences (Bunri Gakubu), but was rejected. It was finally approved as the Faculty of Liberal Arts (Gakugei Gakubu). The application for approval of the Department of Mathematics stated:

> The direct purpose of expanding the Department of Mathematics is to pave the way for women to major in mathematics. However, the expansion is also intended to dispel the common belief that women are unsuited for mathematics and encourage women to pursue their ambitions in the field. The university also hopes to develop research fields particularly suited to women and demonstrate its unique academic style. (Tsuda Juku Rika no rekishi wo kiroku suru kai (ed.) 1987, pp. 115–116)

Although it is unclear what is meant by "fields particularly suited for women," the continuing "segregation" of women's education is clear. Regardless, the specialized education in physics and chemistry offered at Tsuda Juku during the war was never offered at the "true daigaku." Nevertheless, the mathematics department was able to carry on the tradition of science. The wartime science department's laboratory equipment was used to teach natural science-related subjects in the liberal arts courses.

Yoshimura (née Koide) Akashiko (1925–1979), the first graduate of Tsuda Juku's Science Department (Physics and Chemistry), stated:

> When the new university system was introduced, many of the facilities were abolished, as was the case with Tsuda's Department of Physics and Chemistry. It was impossible to equip them with facilities and personnel that met the standards for the establishment of new universities. Some schools, which had been forced to found science and mathematics departments during the war, both regrettably and willingly closed the departments. (Yoshimura Akashiko 1969, p. 19)

Most of the imperial, government, and private universities that had been male dominated became co-educational after the war, allowing women to enroll and study on an equal basis with men.

Conversely, some women's vocational schools became coeducational when they were promoted to universities. For example, Imperial Women's Medical and Pharmaceutical Vocational School and Imperial Women's Vocational School of Science merged to become the coeducational Toho University. Yoshimura saw this as unfortunate from the perspective of women's education, considering that women remained a minority in the sciences and disadvantaged in many ways, even if officially equal. She writes, "It would be nice if more women's universities in the sciences could be established" (ibid.). She believed that the advantage of women's universities was that they were not plagued by gender bias and could develop talent in a relaxed manner. Of women-only universities, only Ochanomizu University, Nara Women's

University (both formerly Women's Higher Normal Schools), and Japan Women's University, established independent science faculties after the war.[8] In the 21st century, Tsuda College established a Department of Information Science in addition to the Department of Mathematics in the Faculty of Liberal Arts, and a Graduate School of Science, comprising a Department of Mathematics and Department of Information Science. The tradition of science has been handed down from generation to generation.

Yoshimura graduated from Tsuda Juku Senmon Gakko in 1947 and enrolled in the Department of Geophysics at the University of Tokyo's Faculty of Science the following year, becoming the first woman in the department. Perhaps her experience of studying with an overwhelming majority of male students – even though it was a co-ed school – until her graduation in 1951 shaped the view expressed in the quotation above. Although primarily a science writer for children, Yoshimura taught history of science at Tsuda College for 18 years from 1956. Her lectures were so popular that she had

---

8 In 1949, Tokyo Women's Higher Normal School became Ochanomizu University, with two faculties: Letters, and Science and Home Economics. In 1950, it restructured, becoming three faculties: Letters and Education, Science, and Home Economics. In 1949, Nara Women's Higher Normal School became Nara Women's University with two faculties: Letters, and Science and Home Economics. In 1953, Science and Home Economics split into distinct faculties. In 1948, Japan Women's University (formerly vocational school) was promoted to the status of university with two faculties: Home Economics, and Letters. Home Economics had two departments: the First Department of Home Economics and Science (majoring in physics and chemistry) and the Second Department of Home Economics and Science (majoring in biology and agriculture). Science became independent from the Faculty of Home Economics in 1992. Four-year women-only universities numbered 32 in 1950, 82 in 1970, 90 in 1990, 96 in 2000, and 76 in 2020 (Mukogawa Josidaigaku Kyoiku Sogo Kenkyusho 2025).

Figure 5.10 Hoshino Ai, the first president of Tsuda College at the Kodaira Campus, March 1951. Courtesy Tsuda University Archives.

to teach in the auditorium. The creation of science historians was a byproduct of Tsuda Juku's science education.[9]

Many of the graduates of the science department found employment as school teachers or researchers. Sato Kimiko (1925–2005), who was Yoshimura's classmate and shared a dormitory room, worked as a laboratory assistant for Sakui

9 While attending Tsuda Juku Senmon Gakko, Yoshimura was highly influenced by Mitsuishi Iwao's lectures and began reading on the history of science. Around the time of her graduation from the University of Tokyo, she worked at the publisher Heibonsha as a contractor to edit the *Kagaku-gijutu-shi nenpyo* [Chronological Table of the History of Science and Technology], where she became acquainted with Nakayama Shigeru (1928–2014), a future historian of science who joined the company (Nakayama graduated in 1951 from the Department of Astronomy, Faculty of Science, the University of Tokyo), and started a study group with Hoshino Yoshiro (1922–2007), a historian of technology (Yoshimura Akashiko wo shinobu kai (ed.) 1980; Yoshimura Mako 2000, pp. 70–72. The former includes obituaries by Nakayama and Hoshino).

Seita (1906–1992) at Tokyo Institute of Technology after graduation. In 1962, she received a doctorate in engineering from Tokyo Institute of Technology based on her thesis entitled "Metallographic Study of Hot Work." She was the first woman to receive a doctorate at Tokyo Institute of Technology and the sixth woman to receive a Doctor of Engineering in Japan.[10] She later continued researching and teaching in metallurgical engineering as a professor at the University of Electro-Communications (Denki Tsushin Daigaku). Tsuda Juku's science department was the starting point for her career (Institute of Science Tokyo Museum and Archives 2025).

The first president of Tsuda College, Hoshino, saw off the last graduates of Tsuda Juku Senmon Gakko in 1951. The following year, she resigned from her position, thus ending her 40-year tenure at Joshi Eigaku Juku, Tsuda Eigaku Juku, Tsuda Juku Senmon Gakko, and Tsuda College. The years she spent running the school were filled with hardships. When the English-focused school was on the brink of collapse during the war, she established a science department, and after the war she turned the school into a women's daigaku. Emulating Umeko's experience of studying science at Bryn Mawr gave Hoshino the confidence to make bold decisions, and the educational system she established nurtured the next generation of human resources. Upon her retirement, Hoshino

---

10 The women who received the Doctor of Engineering by 1962 were: Gobara Sawako (Osaka University, March 25, 1959), Kanno Nobuko (the University of Tokyo, July 27, 1961), Kaminaka Fumiko (Osaka University, February 7, 1962), Shimokobe Chiho (the University of Tokyo, February 12, 1962), Hayashi Masako (the University of Tokyo, March 5, 1962), Sato Kimiko (Tokyo Institute of Technology, March 13, 1962), and Takenaka Haruko (the University of Tokyo, March 31, 1962).

said, “A teacher’s path is sometimes thorny, but I think few lives are as worthwhile as this one” (1955, p. 181). She passed away on December 5, 1972, at the age of 87. Like Umeko, she remained celibate throughout her life.

Epilogue

> It was shortly after the Pacific War and the Japanese people were still hungry and desperately poor in the material sense. But spiritually, my four years in the college dormitory that stood in the Musashino woods of the western Kantō plain were the richest of my life. The students were young and full of rebellious thoughts, each in our own individual way, but we shared an odd devotion to Tsuda Umeko, the founder of our school.
>
> – Oba Minako,
> *Reflections on Tsuda Umeko*, 2021

> If we look carefully at the issue of women and science in essence, we can say without exaggeration that women should be able to study as much as men.
>
> – Kato Sechi,
> "Women and Science," 1940

Hypotheticals may be discouraged in historical scholarship, but when we follow the life of Tsuda Umeko, we cannot help but let our imagination take flight and ask "What if…" at the crossroads of her life. Tsugawa Akiko writes, "If there had been a place for Umeko to work in Japan as a biologist, she might have exerted no small influence on subsequent Japanese women scientists" (2004, p. 97). Umeko returned from the US to Japan in 1892, as she was taking her first steps in the field of biology. To continue her research in Japan, she would have needed the right mentor and research environment. The person with the greatest potential for such a role was Mitsukuri Kakichi, a biology professor at the Imperial University at the time. He was a promising zoologist in his mid-30s who had received his degree from Johns Hopkins University, the alma mater of Umeko's American mentor, Thomas Hunt Morgan. Five years had already passed since the Misaki Marine Biological Station had been established at the Imperial University. As discussed in Chapter 3, Mitsukuri advised Umeko on her research on frog egg development, which Umeko continued after returning to Japan. Had Mitsukuri offered her the opportunity to conduct research at, for example, the Misaki waterfront biological station, and personally supervised her work, she might have achieved notable breakthroughs in zoology. This, of course, presupposes that both Mitsukuri and Umeko possessed the will and desire to pursue such a path, and that those around them could have been persuaded to allow it. Yet none of this came to pass.

Before the war, when science was widely regarded as a male domain, a small number of women scientists emerged. They were often referred to as "*joryu kagakusha*" or "*onna kagakusha*," which literally means "woman scientist" but also conveys a sense of curiosity and strangeness. For instance, in 1935, the magazine *Kagaku Chishiki* (Scientific Knowledge) published a roundtable discussion titled "Asking Women Scientists (*Joryu Kagakusha*)." The magazine defined "women scientists" as "women who research natural science or its applications (1935, p. 307)." The women who were invited included seven with a doctorate in medicine, three with a doctorate in natural science, and one with a doctorate in agriculture.[1] In the public's view, there was no distinction between scientists and medical doctors. This was a common image of "women scientists" during that time.[2]

It was not until after World War II that women in Japan were able to receive the same scientific education as men at universities and pursue careers as scientists. This raises the question of how women were able to take part in the scientific community in Japan before the war, when higher education and research were dominated by men. In many cases, women scientists held teaching positions at preuniversity schools. The first preuniversity schools to offer higher education in the natural sciences to women were Tokyo Women's Higher Normal School and Japan Women's University. Recent findings indicate that the quality of their science education was comparatively high (Nakahara and Ariga 2019; Yamada, 2024; Nihon Joshi Daigaku rigaku kyoiku kenkyukai (ed.) 2013). Mentors (advisors and teachers, often men in the beginning, but not always) encouraged ambitious students to pursue advanced studies at universities that began opening their doors to a few select women after the 1910s. While the teaching posts in the sciences at the preuniversity schools were initially occupied by men, eventually, a few of the best graduates took up posts at their alma maters. The women

---

1 In attendance were Sato Ikuyo, Takeuchi Shigeyo, Yoshihara Ryu, Miyakawa Kanoeko, Toda Kuni, Nakamura Mikae, and Ide Hiro, all of whom were doctors of medicine; Kato Sechi, Yasui Kono, and Kuroda Chika, doctors of science; and Tsujimura Michiyo, a doctor of agriculture. (*Kagaku Chishiki* 1935).

2 The term "*josei kagakusha*" (women scientist or female scientist, which sounds more formal), was used before World War II (e.g., Kato 1940). On the acquisition of doctoral degrees by women before the end of World War II, see Nagashima 1937, and Yamamoto 2006.

who took up these faculty posts became role models for female students to aspire to, leading to the next generation of educators. Thus, a system of post circulation and teacher reproduction for women was gradually created at women's higher normal schools and vocational schools. In the early days, the primary focus of these schools was on instruction rather than research, and they had no research facilities. Therefore, women researchers had to collaborate with external institutions (universities and research institutes), relying on human relationships (Furukawa Yasu 2020, 2024).[3]

For example, Yasui Kono, a first-year science student at Tokyo Women's Higher Normal School, fulfilled her three-year service obligation as a teacher at a girls' high school in Gifu. Then, she re-enrolled in the newly created research program (Kenkyu-ka), to major in biology under Iwakawa Tomotaro and became an assistant professor at her alma mater. Her second mentor was Fujii Kenjiro (1866–1952, botany and genetics) of the Department of Botany, Faculty of Science, Tokyo Imperial University, who privately arranged for her to conduct research at the university's facilities (such as Koishikawa Botanical Garden). She then studied at the University of Chicago and Harvard University (1914–1916). As an overseas fellow of the Ministry of Education, she conducted research on plant tissue under the research title "Science and Domestic Affairs." While studying abroad, she

3 See the following for the history of women scientists in Japan: Yoshimura 1969, 1970, 1971; Yamashita 1983; Tsuda Juku Rika no rekishi wo kisoku suru kai (ed.) 1987, pp. 11–41; Tsugawa and Kanomi 1996; Tsugawa 2004; Iwao and Hara 2007; Saijo 2009; Kodate and Kodate 2016, 2022; and Ogawa 2017. Further research based on primary sources is necessary to provide a more comprehensive overview.

Figure Epilogue 1 Yasui Kono, 1927. The first woman awarded a doctorate of science in Japan submitted her dissertation, "Studies of the Structure of Lignite, Brown Coal, and Bituminous Coal in Japan," to Tokyo Imperial University. Courtesy Ochanomizu University.

took the summer intensive course that Umeko had attended at Woods Hole. After returning to Japan, while working as a professor at Tokyo Women's Higher Normal School, she continued her research in Fujii's laboratory and completed a dissertation on coal tissue (Miki 2004; Nagashima 1937, pp. 4–19; Tsugawa and Kanomi 1996, pp. 33–62). Although she had not received a bachelors' degree, Yasui was awarded a Doctor of Science degree through a system in which the imperial university confers a doctorate after a submitted dissertation is reviewed by a committee. Her students Kuroda Chika (organic chemistry) and Tsujimura Michiyo (1888–1969, agricultural chemistry) became educators and researchers, following Professor Yasui's example; both were later appointed professors at their alma mater. It was the chief researchers (*shunin kenkyuin*) at the Institute for Physical and Chemical Research (Rikagaku Kenkyusho, or RIKEN), founded in 1917, who provided them with research opportunities and guidance as their mentors.[4]

In the process by which Tange Ume (nutritional chemistry), Ohashi Hiro (1882–1973, botany), and Suzuki Hideru (1888–1944, pharmacy) became researchers after graduating from Japan Women's University (a vocational school), we also see the importance of mentors, faculty posts at their alma maters, role models, and the use of outside research facilities.[5] Although these infrastructures were much less developed than they would become after the war, they nevertheless facilitated the professional integration of a modest number of women into the research community in prewar Japan. Regardless, such infrastructures had not yet been established when Tsuda Umeko returned to Japan from Bryn Mawr in the 1890s.

Tange Ume was among the earliest women to gain recognition as a scientist in Japan.[6] She was born in 1873, nine years younger than Umeko, and was almost 40 years-old when her science "career" began. In this sense, one might say

---

4 On Kuroda Chika, see Maeda 1995; Kagawa 1969; Nagashima 1937, pp. 30–41; Tsugawa and Kanomi 1996, pp. 63–94; Kuroda 2019. On Tsujimura Michiyo, see Yamanishi Tei 2007; Yamashita 1983, pp. 71–87; Nagashima 1937, pp. 82–95. On the emergence of women chemists in Japan, see Furukawa Yasu 2024.

5 For Tange Ume, see note 6. On Ohashi Hiro, see Kaneko and Ogawa 2013, and Ohashi 1974. For Suzuki Hideru, see Miyazaki 2013, and Nagashima 1937, pp. 182–191.

6 On Tange Ume, see: Tsuji 1953; Arikawa and Miyazaki 2011; Arikawa and Imaizumi 2013; Arikawa 2017; Nakamura Setsuko 2007; and Yamamoto 2008.

that Umeko was born too early to pursue a scientific career in Japan. The difference between them becomes even clearer when comparing Tange's background with Umeko's. After graduating from Kagoshima Normal School, Tange worked as a teacher at a local elementary school. She entered Japan Women's University as one of the inaugural students in its School of Home Economics in 1901, at the age of 28. The school's educational objective was to "provide Japanese women with appropriate higher education, and to train them to be good wives and wise mothers who are able to adapt to an ever-evolving society and complete their duties" (Tokyo-to (ed.) 1969, p. 58; Kageyama 1994; Kira 2021).[7] Following the philosophy of its founder, Naruse Jinzo, the school emphasized education in the three pillars of domestic science: natural science, spiritual science, and social science. The School offered a high-quality natural science curriculum. Tange was attracted by the chemistry classes given by Nagai Nagayoshi (1845–1929), who had come from Tokyo Imperial University as an adjunct professor at the Kosetsu Chemistry Hall (Kosetsu Kagaku-kan), and worked as Nagai's assistant after graduation. At Nagai's suggestion, Tange took and passed the Ministry of Education's secondary teaching certification exam in chemistry. In 1913, when the Tohoku Imperial University College of Science began admitting women, Tange was accepted with two others. She was 40 years old at the time. She was a so-called "sideline student," meaning that her academic background was other than a high school diploma, which was only awarded to men at the

---

7 For the history of Japan Women's University, see Nihon Joshi Daigakko (ed.) 1942; Nihon Joshi Daigaku (ed.) 2001.

Figure Epilogue 2 Laboratory work at the School of Home Economics in the Kosetsu Chemistry Hall at Japan Women's University. Nagai Nagayoshi is in the center. Students are conducting experiments in *kappogi* (coverall cooking aprons). The Kosetsu Chemistry Hall, completed in 1907 as a gift from Kansai businessman Fujita Denzaburo (founder of the Fujita Zaibatsu), was designed by Nagai based on his experience studying in Germany. It was equipped with a chemistry lecture room, laboratory, preparation room, balance room, specimen room, and library, and was comparable to the facilities at the Imperial University. Courtesy the Naruse Memorial Hall, Japan Women's University.

time. At the university, she conducted chemical research on persimmon tannin under the guidance of the notable organic chemist Majima Riko (1874–1962), who became her second mentor. After graduation she remained in Majima's laboratory as the first woman graduate student in Japan. Later, as a commissioned researcher for the Ministry of Education and the Ministry of Home Affairs, she went to the US to study nutritional chemistry under the title "Research on Social Facilities for Science Education and Child Nutrition," and in 1927, at the age of 54, she received a Ph.D. from Johns Hopkins University. After returning to Japan, at the age of 57, she became a professor at Japan Women's University and joined the laboratory of Suzuki Umetaro (1874–1943), who

Figure Epilogue 3 Tange Ume conducting an experiment at RIKEN. While employed as a professor at Japan Women's University, she also conducted vitamin research in Suzuki Umetaro's laboratory at RIKEN as a contract researcher (*shokutaku*). She received a Ph.D. from Johns Hopkins University in 1927. In Japan, she was awarded a doctorate in agriculture from Tokyo Imperial University in 1940 for her research on vitamin B_2 complex.

became her third mentor at RIKEN, to conduct research on vitamin B_2. Tange's research was published mostly in the RIKEN Bulletin (*RIKEN Iho*) and *Scientific Papers*, as well as in research conferences held at RIKEN.

Tange's professional path as a female scientist was not straightforward. Like Umeko, she had no role model to follow. Unlike Umeko, however, Tange had three mentors in Japan, as well as opportunities to conduct research. It was a circuitous path, but as a chemistry teacher, Tange was able to remain close to her alma mater, teach, serve as a role model, and become a mentor herself, paving the way for the next generation of students. Thus, the environment and infrastructure behind the project had changed dramatically between the 1890s, when Umeko returned home, and the 1920s, when Tange began her research activities. This reveals that the status of a scientist is not simply the product of individual talent and effort, but is also socially constructed.

Nevertheless, the social differences between the two eras were not simply a gift from above; they occurred through the active efforts of women with a burning desire to learn, in a variety of situations. After graduating from the science department of Tokyo Women's Higher Normal School, Kato Sechi (1893–1999, physical chemistry) made a personal plea to enter Hokkaido Imperial University, resulting in the opportunity to study as a "full elective student" and later joined RIKEN, where she became the first woman chief researcher after the war. In 1940, in an essay titled "Women and Science," she wrote to women who aspired to become scientists,

> We should not wait for the coming of the time to be given to us in vain. If you knock, the back door will open. If you make an effort to break in, a small desk will be given to you. If you are grateful for what you have been given and devote yourself to learning with all your heart and soul, you will gradually shine. (1940, p. 104)[8]

The accumulation of such efforts resulted in changes to the system. Sawayanagi Masataro (1865–1927), the first president of Tohoku Imperial University, recognized a small number of inquisitive women and decided that the university must open its doors to these "unfortunate women who must become independent" (Sawayanagi 1924, p. 299; Yukawa 2003, pp. 50–72; Fujiwara 1998). Although it met friction from the

---

8 Kato continues, "In many cases, an easy environment does not allow a person to grow as much as she would like. I am by no means satisfied with today's

Ministry of Education, it subsequently set a precedent for other imperial universities to allow the admission of women.

Umeko secretly studied biology at the government's expense. Yet, as noted earlier, even in the generation of Tange and Yasui, the government discriminated against women scientists who had studied abroad on government sponsorship; sponsored women were not permitted to pursue research in the pure natural sciences. When Kuroda Chika received a government scholarship to study at Oxford University in 1921, she was instructed that the purpose of her study should be "scientific research related to housework." Nevertheless, she pursued pure organic chemistry, investigating the chemical structure of the pigment of purple root. The Ministry of Education's directive reflected gender bias, permitting women to study abroad only for research related to housework, nutrition, and foodstuffs. In this era of strict gender norms, there was also a "segregation (*sumiwake*)" of research topics deemed suitable for women in the sciences, as limiting their fields of inquiry made it easier to avoid unnecessary friction and obtain approval. Just as many early women doctors were obstetricians, gynecologists, or nutritional consultants, some women scientists chose to pursue research in nutritional chemistry and food science, or other fields related to the home

---

social environment for women. However, frankly speaking, I was grateful for the fact that I had to work twice or thrice as hard to survive." (1940, p. 104)

Kato, who worked at RIKEN for a long time, said, "Women were my special favorite," and took the initiative in hiring women as collaborators and research assistants in her laboratory (1978, p. 80).

On Kato Sechi, see Maeda 2004; and Yamamoto 2017. On women scientists at RIKEN, see Rikagaku Kenkyusho 100 nenshi henshu iinkai (ed.) 2018, Part 2, Chapter 5.

and household.[9] Despite this "self-limitation," many women – such as Tange, Tsujimura, and Kuroda – made remarkable academic contributions in their respective fields.

A notable attribute of the early women scientists is their marital status. A significant proportion of these individuals, including Tange, Yasui, Kuroda, Tsujimura, Ohashi, and Suzuki Hideru, were unmarried. I conducted a biographical survey using prosopography (collective biographical analysis) of some 70 female scientific researchers born before 1920 and found that 75% of them were single. This illustrates the difficulty for married women to pursue careers in science, as well as the magnitude of the spirit of inquiry of these women who devoted themselves to academia as lifelong celibates. (Furukawa Yasu 2020).

In the fall of 2014, I gave a lecture titled "Tsuda Umeko and Biology" at the "Symposium on the 150th Anniversary of Tsuda Umeko's Birth," held in conjunction with Tsuda University's Homecoming Day. Afterwards, someone asked, "What would have happened if Ms. Tsuda had stayed in the US after studying at Bryn Mawr?" (Furukawa Yasu 2014). This is a fascinating question that stirs the imagination. I am certain that her prospects for a career as a scientific researcher would

9 Watanabe Yoko divides women professionals in modern Japan into several categories: "women-entering professionals" (*i.e.*, those in fields originally considered male professions in which women entered later) include doctors, scientists, and engineers. The phenomenon of "segregation" is pointed out as one of the early characteristics of this category (2014, Ch. IV, Section 3). Tange Ume says, "The reason I decided to pursue this kind of study was because I realized that women and food have a very close relationship" (*Yomiuri Shimbun*, 1921). Suzuki Umetaro, who supervised Tange at RIKEN, said, "Women are interested in nutrition from the instinct to bring up their children. It can be said that a mother's desire to bring up her children well has brought nutritional chemistry to the present day" (*Yomiuri Shimbun*, 1943).

have been much better had she remained in the United States than if she had returned to her home country. In the US, there were strong mentors and favorable institutional structures. As discussed in Chapter 3, one can imagine that Umeko, whose talents were highly regarded at Bryn Mawr College, would have first been transferred from special student status to undergraduate status and graduated with a bachelor's degree. She then would have received a scholarship to a graduate program to further her research in embryology under Morgan and received her Ph.D. She might have become Morgan's assistant and eventually obtained a post at a university. Alice M. Boring, who was a student alongside Umeko at Bryn Mawr, became a professor at Mount Holyoke College, and Ida Hyde, who worked with Umeko as a laboratory assistant, became a professor at the University of Kansas. Morgan was invited to Columbia University in 1904 and conducted research on mutations in *Drosophila*, which led to the Nobel Prize in Physiology or Medicine; if he had taken Umeko, they might have collaborated on that work. In any case, if Umeko had severed her ties with Japan and stayed in the US to pursue her career as a biologist, she might have found success despite the difficulties and hardships. She could have been a role model for Japanese women as a female scientist across the Pacific.[10]

After giving that answer, I addressed the alumnae in the lecture hall:

---

10 Nakazawa Shingo pondered: "I wonder what would have happened if Tsuda Umeko had continued her zoologist's career as it was. If she had continued her research in collaboration with Morgan, she would probably have become a great zoologist on par with Morgan, as we can imagine from her later activities" (Nakazawa 1988, p. 48).

> If I may add one more thing, if Umeko had stayed in the US, there would have been no Joshi Eigaku Juku. That means there would have been no Tsuda University! This means that you would all have led completely different lives. I am here today with my fellow alumni, holding this symposium and having this conversation, because Umeko chose to return to Japan after much hesitation at that time.

If one evaluates Umeko solely in terms of her contribution to the development of biology or her influence on women scientists, her score would probably be low. Although this book is a biography of Tsuda Umeko from the perspective of the history of science, it was not my intention to evaluate Umeko from that perspective. This book focuses on the meaning of her encounter with natural sciences in the US, the conflicts and feuds she faced, and the creative process she went through. She spent her formative years in the US in the late 19th century and was shocked by the gender order in Japan upon her return. I have explored the scientific education she received at Bryn Mawr College, and how her experience of research in natural science, which was forbidden to women at Peeresses' School, affected her life as an English teacher, and how she applied it to the education of Japanese women in the social context of the time. I have described how Umeko's legacy was passed on and how it bore fruit, from the perspectives of the history of science and gender. Through an in-depth look at Umeko's career, the book illuminates the question of what it means to be a female scientist.

It also raises the question of why someone as strong-willed and dynamic as Umeko did not strive to forge a path as a Japanese woman in science. As discussed in Chapter 3,

Umeko did not publicly reveal that she had majored in biology at Bryn Mawr during her lifetime. It seems that Umeko's past as a biologist became known to the public only after her death, when Yoshikawa Toshikazu published *Tsuda Umeko* (1930). Ultimately, it is more accurate to say that Umeko chose the path of educating Japanese women in English for herself as more suitable than to say she abandoned natural science. As Anna Hartshorne, who helped with the school administration, recalls, Umeko had science education in mind when she established the school, but realized that it would be impossible to establish science as a department due to financial difficulties. Thus, she founded a women's English school and devoted the latter half of her life to teaching English and running the school. Umeko emphasized that English was not the end goal. Rather, she believed that teaching English to Japanese women would open their eyes to the Western world, thought, learning, and science, and would awaken them to the barriers and gender inequalities in patriarchal Japanese society. It is from this perspective that Umeko chose her career as an English teacher. These thoughts matured and were internalized during Umeko's experiences at Bryn Mawr. Hence, when discussing her life as an educator, we cannot ignore Umeko's relationship with science.

Umeko dreamt of the Joshi Eigaku Juku eventually evolving into a "true daigaku." She may have thought that scientific education would be offered at that time. Half a century later, Umeko's dream was realized through the dedicated efforts of her successor, Hoshino Ai, and others. Hoshino, who taught English language and literature at the school, had followed in Umeko's footsteps of a scientific education at Bryn Mawr. When English was regarded as a hostile language during the war and the school, which had focused on English education, faced a crisis of survival, Hoshino quickly overcame the crisis by creating mathematics, and physics and chemistry departments, leading to the birth of the new Tsuda College immediately after the war. What Hoshino achieved reached far beyond the confines of Tsuda College. She also played a pioneering role in establishing "true" women's universities – institutions of higher learning for women once deemed unimaginable in prewar Japan. Hence, the evaluation of Umeko's contributions should extend beyond her own lifetime, encompassing the legacy she bequeathed, the traditions she established, and the impact she exerted on subsequent generations.

Bibliography

Archival Sources

Tsuda University Archives

Resume of Tsuda Umeko, September 1885.

Frederic Lee's letter of introduction for Umeko Tsuda, dated February 27, 1891.

Bryn Mawr College Record of Ume Tsuda, 1889–1892 (hand-written notebook of course transcripts with the teachers' signatures).

"The Orientation of the Frog's Egg," pt. II, manuscript written by Umeko Tsuda, 1892.

Letter from Leah Goff to Umeko Tsuda, January 24, 1893.

Letter from Mitsukuri Kakichi to Umeko Tsuda, dated March 25, 1893.

Draft letter from Umeko Tsuda to Mitsukuri Kakichi, no date.

Draft letter from Umeko Tsuda to Thomas H. Morgan, July 25, 1893.

Letter from Thomas H. Morgan to Umeko Tsuda, October 14, 1893.

Letter from Thomas H. Morgan to Umeko Tsuda, February 4, 1926.

Tsuda Umeko, untitled Romanized manuscript (matters related to her study in the U.S.), no date (six pages).

M. Carey Thomas, "Address given by President Thomas of Bryn Mawr College, July 8th, 1915" (manuscript of speech given by Thomas at Joshi Eigaku Juku).

Anna C. Hartshorne, memoranda, December 13, 1933; November 16, 1940; and no date.

Bryn Mawr College Special Collections

Umé Tsuda, Transcript, 1889–1892.

Bryn Mawr College, *Trustee's Minutes,* dated October 9, 1891.

M. Carey Thomas' letter of introduction for Ume Tsuda, dated May 27, 1892.

Letter from Umé Tsuda to Carey Thomas, dated August 9, 1900.

Ai Hoshino, Transcript 1908–1912.

Gakushuin Archives

Tsuda Umeko, "Jishoku negai-sho [Application for Resignation]," April 30, 1889, in *Kazoku Jogakko shintai roku, Meiji 18 nen to 30 nen* [Peeresses' School Records of Appointment and Resignation, 1885–1897].

Kitazawa Masanari to the principal of Peeresses' School and others, June 22, 1891, *Kazoku Jogakko shintai roku, Meiji 18 nen to 30 nen* [Peeresses' School Records of Appointment and Resignation, 1885–1897].

Tsuda Sen, "Kicho enki negai [Request for Extension of Return]," May 27, 1892, *Kazoku Jogakko shintai roku, Meiji 18 nen to 30 nen* [Peeresses' School Records of Appointment and Retirement, 1885–1897].

Imperial Household Archives, Imperial Household Agency

"Kazoku Jogakko gakka ni tsuki goshinyu [Imperial Instructions on the Curriculum of Peeresses' School]," Motoda Nagazane shuki [Motoda Nagazane Memorandum], in *Motoda danshaku-ke bunsho* [Baron Motoda Family Documents] 17, July 25, 1885.

Tsuda Umeko, "Negai-sho [Application]" to Hijikata Hisamitsu, dated May 9, 1888, Tsuda Umeko file in *Naiji-ka shintai-roku, Meiji 22 nen* [Internal Affairs Section, Records of Appointment and Resignation, 1889].

Tsuda Umeko, "Ryugaku enki negai [Application for Extension of Study]," dated June 15, 1891, *Naiji-ka shintai-roku, Meiji 24 nen* [Internal Affairs Section, Records of Appointment and Resignation, 1891].

Nishimura Shigeki to Hijikata Hisamitsu, "No. 40," dated June 15, 1891, *Naiji-ka Shintai-roku, Meiji 24 nen* [Internal Affairs Section, Records of Appointment and Resignation, 1891].

American Association of University Women, Washington, DC, Archives

Ida Hyde, "Before Women Were Human Beings: A Woman from Dark Ages," (manuscript) 1931, revised 1938, Ida Hyde Papers.

Marine Biological Laboratory Library

Ida Hyde, paper presented at the San Diego Federation Club as the representative of A.A.U.W., 1924 (manuscript), Ida Hyde Collection.

New York State University, Oswego, Penfield Library Special Collections

"Summary of Reports of the Superintendents and Teachers for the term ending June 30, 1891," *Grade Reports 7/1889–7/1895*, 17/1/5.

Vassar College Libraries Archives and Special Collections

Transcript of Sutematz Yamakawa, A.B.1882, Registrar's Office.

Letters from Sutematz Yamakawa to Alice Bacon, dated August 2, 1882; January 18, February 3, and February 20, 1883, Oyama Collection.

Other Sources

Aiya, Sakae (1929), "Tsuda no o-Ume-san [Tsuda Ume-san]," *Eigo Seinen* (The Rising Generation), vol. 62, no. 4, pp. 139–140.

Akiyama, Hisa (1985), "Meiji-shoki joshi ryugaku-sei no shogai: Yamakawa Suetmatsu no baai [The Life of a Woman Foreign Student in the Early Meiji Period: The Case of Yamakawa Sutematsu]," *Ronshu* (Kobe College Studies, Kobe College Research Institute), vol. 31, no. 3, pp. 81–104.

Allen, Gerland E. (1970a), "Wilson, Edmund Beecher," *Dictionary of Scientific Biography*, vol. XIV, New York: Scribner, pp. 423–436.

Allen, Gerland E. (1970b), "Morgan, Thomas Hunt," *Dictionary of Scientific Biography*, vol. IX, New York: Scribner, pp. 515–526.

Amano, Ikuo (2009), *Daigaku no Tanjo: Daigaku eno chosen* [The Birth of the University: The Challenge to the University], Tokyo: Chuko Shinsho.

Aoyama, Nao (1949), *Yasui Tetsu den* [Biography of Yasui Tetsu], Tokyo: Yasui Tetsu den kanko iinkai.

Arikawa, Yoshiko (2017), "Michi naki michi wo: Josei kagakusha no paionia Tange Ume [Off the Beaten Path: The Pioneer Women Chemist Tange Ume], *Kagakushi koen kenshu kai siryou* (Proceedings of the History of Chemistry Lecture), no. 14, pp. 6–17.

Arikawa, Yoshiko and Imaizumi Sachiko (2013), "Tange Ume: Josei kagakusha no michi wo hiraku [Tange Ume: Paving the Way for Women Scientists]," in Nihon Joshi Daigaku rigaku kyoiku kenkyukai (ed.) 2013, pp. 55–76.

Arikawa, Yoshiko and Miyazaki Akane (2011), *Shiraume no yooni: Kagakusha Tange Ume no kiseki* [Like a White Plum Tree: In the Footsteps of the Chemist Tange Ume], Tokyo: Kagaku Kogyo Nipposha.

Bacon, Alice Mabel (1891), *Japanese Girls and Women*, Boston and New York: Houghton, Mifflin and Co.

Bacon, Alice Mabel (1893), *A Japanese Interior*, Boston and New York: Houghton, Mifflin and Co.

Boring, Alice (1946), "Thomas Hunt Morgan," *Alumnae Bulletin* (Bryn Mawr College), February, pp. 18–19.

Brush, Stephen G. (1978) "Nettie M. Stevens and the Discovery of Sex Determination by Chromosomes," *Isis*, vol. 69, pp. 163–172.

Bryn Mawr College (1890a, 1891a, 1892a), *Bryn Mawr College Program*, Philadelphia: Bryn Mawr College.

Bryn Mawr College (1889, 1890b, 1891b, 1892b, 1893), *The President's Report to the Board of Trustees*, Philadelphia: Bryn Mawr College.

Bryn Mawr College (1912), *Bryn Mawr College Calendar*, Philadelphia: Bryn Mawr College.

Darwin, Charles (1876), *The Effects of Cross and Self Fertilisation in the Vegetable Kingdom*, London: John Murray.

Denda, Isao (1962), *Kindai Nihon nosei shiso no kenkyu: Nihon no kindaika to chiho keizai* [A Study of Thoughts on Agricultural Policy in Modern Japan: Japan's Modernization and Local Economy], Tokyo: Miraisha.

Dobutsugaku Zasshi (1910), "Mitsukuri Kakichi hakase kinengo [Special Issue of Dr. Mitukuri Kakichi]," *Dobutsugaku Zasshi* (Zoological Journal), vol. 22, no. 256.

Dobutsugaku Zasshi (1935), "Ko-Ishikawa Chiyomatsu hakase kinengo [Memorial Volume of the Late Dr. Ishikawa Chiyomatsu]," *Dobutsugaku Zasshi* (Zoological Journal). vol. 47.

Doke, Tatsumasa (1996), "Wagakuni no kagakushi: Nihon Kagakushi Gakkai no sosetu [History of Science in Japan: The Founding of the History of Science Society of Japan]," *Gakujutu no Doko* (Academic Trends), vol. 1, no. 1, pp. 58–62.

Fujita Taki-sensei no ronshu to omoide sewanin-kai (Association of Caretakers of Fujita Taki-sensei's Essays and Memories) (ed.) (1993), *Arigatou: Fujita Taki-sensei no ronshu to omoide* [Thank You: Fijita Taki-sensei's Essays and Memories], Tokyo: Domesu Shuppan.

Fujita, Taki (1943), "Rika kinkyo [Recent Situation of the Science Department]," *Kaiho* (Bulletin for the Tsuda Eigaku Juku Alumni Association), no. 55 (December), pp. 8–12.

Fujita, Taki (1971), *Waga michi: Kokoro no deai* [My Way: Meeting with Minds], Tokyo: Domesu Shuppan.

Fujiwara, Masahiro (1998), "Kyusei daigaku ni okeru josei jukosha no juyo to sono tenkai [The Acceptance and Development of Female Students in the Old System Universities]," *Kyoikugaku Zasshi* (Journal of Educational Research, Nihon University), no. 32, pp. 76–91.

Fukui, Yuriko (2000), "Tokyo Daigaku Dobutugaku Kyoshitu ni okeru sotsugyo ronbun: Dai ikki sotsugyo (1881 nen) kara Yatsu Naohide no taikan (1938 nen) made [Graduation Theses in the Department of Zoology, University of Tokyo: From the First Graduation (1881) to Yatsu Naohide's Retirement (1938)]," *Seibutsugakushi Kenkyu* (The Japanese Journal of the History of Biology), no. 65, pp. 83–101.

Furukawa, Haruo (1941), "'Siiboruto kenkyu' eno hoi [Addendum to the 'Siebold Studies'," *Kagakusi Kenkyu* (Journal of History of Science, Japan), no. 1, pp. 147–148.

Furukawa, Yasu (2010), "Tsuda Umeko to seibutsugaku: Kagakushi to Jendaa no shiten kara [Tsuda Umeko and Biology: From the Perspective of History of Science and Gender]," *Kagakusi kenkyu* (Journal of History of Science, Japan), vol. 49, pp. 12–21.

Furukawa, Yasu (2014), "Tsuda Umeko to seibutsugaku [Tsuda Umeko and Biology]," a lecture presented at the Symposium Commemorating the 150th Anniversary of the Birth of Tsuda Umeko, "Umi wo watatte: Umeko, Sutematsu no sensinsei [Sailing the Sea: Umeko and Sutematsu's Progressiveness]," Tsuda University.

Furukawa, Yasu (2018), *Kagaku no shakai-shi: Runessansu kara 20 seiki made* [A Social History of Science: From the Renaissance to the 20th Century], Tokyo: Chikuma Shobo.

Furukawa, Yasu (2020), "Nihon ni okeru josei kagakusha no tanjo: Senzen-ki kenkyusha no keireki kara no ichi kosatsu [The Birth of Women Scientists in Japan: A Study from the Biographies of Researchers in the Prewar Period]," Kayo zemi (Tuesday Seminar on the History of Science, Tokyo Institute of Technology) (oral presentation).

Furukawa, Yasu (2024), "The Emergence of Women Chemists in Prewar Japan," *Kagakushi* (Journal of the Japanese Society for the History of Chemistry), vol. 51, no. 3, pp. 165–181.

Furuki, Yoshiko (1991), *The While Plum: A Biography of Ume Tsuda,*

New York and Tokyo: Weatherhill.

Furuki, Yoshiko (1992), *Tsuda Umeko*, Tokyo: Shimizu Shoin.

Gakushuin Hyaku nenshi hensan iinkai (Gakushuin Centennial History Editorial Committee) (ed.) (1981), *Gakushuin hyaku nenshi* [Gakushuin Centennial History], Part 1, Tokyo: Gakushuin.

Gakushuin Joshi Chuto-ka and Koto-ka (Gakushuin Girls' Secondary and High School) (ed.) (1985), *Gakushuin Joshi Chuto-ka and Koto-ka hyaku nenshi* [A Centennial History of Gakushuin Girls' Secondary and High School], Tokyo: Gakushuin Joshi Chuto-ka and Koto-ka.

Gardiner, Mary S. (1951), "David Hilt Tennent, 1873–1941," *National Academy of Sciences Biographical Memoirs*, Vol. XXVI, pp. 98–119.

Goto, Arata (2019), "Kindai nihon ni okeru kinshu undo: 1890 nen Tokyo Kinshu Kai no seiritsu made [The Temperance Movement in Modern Japan: Toward the Establishment of the Tokyo Temperance Association in 1890]," *Hosei Ronso* (The Review of Legal and Political Sciences, Hosei Uiversity), vol. 55, no. 1, pp. 15–28.

Hanami, Sakumi (ed.) (1939), *Danshaku Yamakawa-sensei den* [Biography of Baron Yamakawa-Sensei], Tokyo: Ko-Yamakawa Danshaku Kinen-kai.

Hara, Michinori (1994), "Ine no zosan ni hachimitsu: Meiji zenki no shiken tenmatsu [Honey for Increased Rice Production: A Story of Experiments in the Early Meiji Era]," *Mitsubachi Kagaku* (Bee Science), vol. 15, no. 3, pp. 125–130.

Hartshorne, Anna C. (1929), "The Years of Preparation: A Memory of Ume Tsuda," reproduced in Tsuda Juku Daigaku (ed.) 1984, pp. 512–517.

Hatanaka, Rie (2004), *Taisho-ki joshi koto kyoiku shi no kenkyu: Keihanshin wo chushin ni site* [A Study of the History of Women's Higher Education in the Taisho Period: Focusing on the Keihanshin Area], Tokyo: Kazama Shobo.

Hayashi, Makoto (2000), "*Dobutsugaku Zasshi* shoki no mokuteki to seika: Meiji-jidai Nihon ni okeru dobutsugaku kenkyu no ichi danmen [The Purpose and Results of the Early Years of the *Zoological Journal*: A Cross-Section of Zoological Research in Meiji Japan]," *Seibutsugakushi Kenkyu* (The Japanese Journal of the History of Biology), no. 66, pp. 1–13.

Hayashi, Makoto (2001), "1890 nendai ni okeru Nihon no dobutsu gakusha no ronbun happyo ni tsuite [On the Publication of Papers by Japanese Zoologists in the 1890s]," *Seibutsugakushi Kenkyu* (The Japanese Journal of the History of Biology), no. 68, pp. 45–56.

Hiratsuka, Raicho (1971), *Genshi, josei wa taiyo de atta: Hiratsuka Raicho jiden* [Originally Women Were the Sun: The Autobiography of Hiratsuka Raicho], Part 1, Tokyo: Otsuki Shoten.

Hiroi, Tazuko (2021), "Shimoda Utako wo torae naosu [Reconsidering Shimoda Utako]," in Hiroi (ed.) 2021, pp. 317–329.

Hiroi, Tazuko (ed.) (2021), *Shimoda Utako to kindai nihon: Ryosai-kenbo-ron to josei kyoiku no soshutsu* [Shimoda Utako and Modern Japan: The Theory of Good Wife and Wise Mother and the Creation of Women's Education], Tokyo: Keiso Shobo.

Hollis, Andrew P. (1898), *The Contribution of the Oswego Normal School to Educational Progress in the United States*, Boston: D.C. Heath.

Horowitz, Helen L. (1999), *The Power and Passion of M. Carey Thomas*, Urbana and Chicago: University of Illinois Press.

Hoshino, Ai (1943), "Shin gakka zosetsu ni tsuite [On the Establishment of the New Department]," *Kaiho* (Tsuda Eigaku Juku Alumni Association Bulletin), no. 54 (February), pp. 1–7.

Hoshino, Ai (1955), "Ichi kyoshi no ayumi: Gakusei to tomoni 40 nen [The Path of a Teacher: 40 Years with Students]," *Seikai Orai*, vol. 21, no. 1, pp. 178–181.

Hoshino, Ai (1990), *Shoden* [A Brief Autobiography], Tokyo: Oozorasha.

Hotta, Kunimoto (2016), *Diskabaa Okami Kei* [Discover Okami Kei], Private publication.

Hyde, Ida H. (1938), "Before Women Were Human Beings: Adventures of an American Fellow in German Universities of the '90s," *Journal of the American Association of University Women*, vol. 31, no.4, pp. 226–236.

Iino, Masako, Kameda Kinuko and Takahashi Yuko (eds.) (2000), *Tsuda Umeko wo sasaeta hitobito* [The People Who Supported Tsuda Umeko], Tokyo: Yuhikaku.

Ikuta, Sumie (2003), *Butoh eno shotai: Nihon saisho no joshi ryugakusei Nagai Shigeko no shogai* [Invitation to Butoh: The Life of Japan's First Female Student Studying Abroad, Nagai Shigeko], Tokyo, Bungei-sha.

Ikuta, Sumie (2017), *Uryu Shigeko: Mo hitori no joshi ryugakusei* [Uryu Shigeko: Another Foreign Woman Student], Tokyo: 22 Seiki Art. A revised edition of Ikuta (2003).

Imai, Mitsuaki (ed.) (1992), *Amerika kaseigaku zenshi: Biicha kara Richaazu e domesutikku feminizumu no shiso* [Prehistory of American Home Economics: From Beecher to Richards, Domestic Feminist Thought], Tokyo: Koseikan.

Institute of Science Tokyo Museum and Archives (2025), "Rikejo no sendatsu tachi [Rikejo; Japan's Pioneering Women in Science]," https://www.titech.ac.jp/public-relations/about/stories/researchpioneer-rikejo, accessed October 1, 2025.

Ishii, Runa (2000), "Sengo nihon no joshi kotokyoiku kaikakuni okeru josei riidaa no yakuwari: Hoshino Ai wo chusin toshite [The Role of Women Leaders in the Reform of Women's Higher Education in Postwar Japan: Focusing on Hoshino Ai]," *Kokusai Gaku Review* (The Review of International Studies, J. F. Oberlin University), no. 12, pp. 67–83.

Isono, Naohide (1985), "Tokyo daigaku rigakubu dobutsugaku kyoshitu no rekisi [History of the Department of Zoology, Faculty of Science, University of Tokyo]," in Takewaki Kiyoshi (ed.), *Mizukamakiri wa tobu: Ichi dobutsugakusha no kiseki* [Ranatra Chinensis Flies: The Trajectory of a Zoologist], Tokyo: Gakkai Shuppan Center, pp. 139–217.

Ito, Kenji (2015, 2016), "'Ronbun' no nai kagakusha, Kuwaki Ayao [A Scientist without 'Papers', Kuwaki Ayao], *Kyuri* (Physics), (I) no. 1, pp. 40–27; (2) no. 2, pp. 39–47; and (3) no. 3, pp. 44–51.

Iwao, Sumiko and Hara Hiroko (eds.) (2007), *Kagaku suru kokoro: Nihon no josei kagakusha tachi* [The Scientific Spirit: Women Scientists in Japan], Tokyo: Nikkan Kogyo Shimbunsha.

Jogaku Zasshi (1894), "Tsuda Ume-jo no seibutsugaku jo no hakken [The Biological Discovery of Miss Tsuda Ume]," *Jogaku Zasshi* (Education of Women Magazine), vol. 7, no. 387, p. 693.

Joshi Gakushuin (ed.) (1935), *Joshi Gakushuin 50 nenshi* [A 50 Year-History of Joshi Gakushuin], Tokyo: Joshi Gakushuin.

Kagaku Chishiki (1935), "Zadankai: Joryu kagakusha ni kiku [Roundtable Discussion: Asking Women Scientists," *Kagaku Chishiki* (Scientific Knowledge), vol. 15, no. 9, pp. 307–314.

Kagawa Jinken Kenkyusho (Kagawa Institute for Human Rights Studies) (ed.) (2006), *Yasui Kono: Nihon hatsu no josei hakase* [Yasui Kono: Japan's First Female Doctor], Marugame: Kagawa Jinken Kenkyusho.

Kagawa, Michiko (1969), "Josei kagakusha no senku: Kuroda Chika [A Pioneer of Women Scientists: Kuroda Chika]," *Shizen* (Nature), (January), pp. 60–63.

Kagawa, Setsuko (2021), "Shimoda Utako to Tsuda Umeko: Seiyo bunka tono deai to joshi kyoiku no soshutsu [Shimoda Utako and Tsuda Umeko: Encounter with Western Culture and the Creation of Women's Education]," in Hiroi (ed.) 2021, pp. 87–117.

Kageyama, Reiko (1994), *Naruse Jinzo no kyoiku shiso: Naruse-teki puragumatizumu to Nihon Joshi Daigakko ni okeru kyoiku* [The Educational Thought of Naruse Jinzo: Naruse-style Pragmatism and Education at Japan Women's University], Tokyo: Kazama Shobo.

Kaigo, Tokiomi (1981), *Kaigo Tokiomi chosaku-shu* [Collected Writings of Kaigo Tokiomi], vol. 10, Tokyo: Tokyo Shoseki.

Kaigo, Tokiomi (ed.) (1962), *Rinji kyoiku kaigi no kenkyu* [A Study of the Provisional Education Conference], Tokyo: Tokyo Daigaku Shuppankai.

Kameda, Kinuko (2000), "Uryu Shigeko: Seishun wo tomoni shita tomo to shite [Uryu Shigeko: As a Friend Who Shared Youth]," in Iino et al. (eds.) 2000, pp. 71–96.

Kameda, Kinuko (2005), *Tsuda Umeko: Hitori no meikyoshi no kiseki* [Tsuda Umeko: The Path of a Renowned Teacher], Tokyo: Sobunsha Shuppan.

Kameda, Kinuko (2006), *Tsuda Umeko to Ana Haazuhon: Futakumi no oyako no monogatari* [Tsuda Umeko and Anna Hartshorne: A Tale of Two Pairs of Father and Daughter], Tokyo: Sobunsha Shuppan.

Kamichika, Ichiko (1972), *Kamichika Ichiko jiden: Waga ai waga tatakai* [The Autobiography of Kamichika Ichiko: My Love and My Strife], Tokyo: Kodansha.

Kaneko, Takako and Ogawa Kyoko (2013), "Ohashi Hiro: Seibutsu gakusha kara dai 5dai gakucho e [Ohashi Hiro: From Biologist to the Fifth President]," in Nihon Joshi Daigaku rigaku kyoiku kenkyukai (ed.) 2013, pp. 77–98.

Kano, Hirokatsu (2018), "Tsuda Sen no Nogyo Zasshi to chiiki eno hirogari: Meiji 10 nendai to 20 nendai no dokusha ni chumoku shite [Tsuda Sen's *Nogyo Zasshi* (Agricultural Journal) and its Spread to the Regions: Focusing on Readers in the Meiji 10s and 20s]," *Kokusai Kankeigaku Kenkyu* (The Study of International Relations, Tsuda College), vol. 45, pp. 1–17.

Katayama, Hiroshi (1929), "Tsuda Umeko joshi no omoide [Reminiscences of Ms.Tsuda Umeko]," *Eigo Seinen* (The Rising Generation), vol. 62, no. 4, p. 138.

Kato, Kyosuke (1955), *Toho Daigaku 30 nenshi* [A Thirty-Year History of Toho University], Tokyo: Toho University.

Kato, Sechi (1940), "Josei to kagaku [Women and Science]," *Kagaku Chishiki* (Scientific Knowledge), vol. 20, no. 4, pp. 102–104.

Kato, Sechi (1978), "Mimizu no tawagoto [Worm's Nonsense Talk]," *Shizen* (Nature), special issue of 60-year history of RIKEN, vol. 33, no. 13, pp. 78–80.

Kawamoto, Shizuko (2001a), "Hajime ni [Introduction]," in Kawamoto et al. 2001, pp. 9–16.

Kawamoto, Shizuko (2001b), "Hoshino Ai: 'Tsuda-sensei no gakko' wo mamori nuku [Hoshino Ai: Protecting and Preserving 'Tsuda-sensei's School']," in Kawamoto et al. 2001, pp. 19–27.

Kawamoto Shizuko (2001c), "Yamakawa Kikue: Fujin kaiho-ron no paionia [Yamakawa Kikue: Pioneer of Women's Liberation Theory]," in Kawamoto et al. 2001, pp. 28–35.

Kawamoto, Shizuko, Kameda Kinuko and Takakuwa Yoshiko (2001), *Tsuda Umeko no musume tachi: Hito-tsubu no shushi kara* [Tsuda Umeko's Daughters: From a Single Seed], Tokyo: Domesu Shuppan.

Kazoku shiryo kenkyukai (Peerage Documents Study Group) (ed.) (2011), *Kazoku reijo tachi no Taisho/Showa* [The Taisho and Showa Periods of Peerage Daughters], Tokyo: Yoshikawa Kobunkan.

Keenan, Katherine (1983), "Lilian Vaughan Morgan (1870–1952): Her Life and Work," *American Zoology*, vol. 23, pp. 867–876.

Kega, Takeo (2014), *Aoyama Gakuin no rekishi wo sasaeta hitobito*

[People Who Supported the History of Aoyama Gakuin], Tokyo: Aoyama Gakuin.

Kihara, Hitoshi, Shinoto Yoshito, and Isono Naohide (eds.) (1988), *Kindai Nihon seibutsugakusha shoden* [Brief Biographies of Biologists in Modern Japan], Tokyo: Hirakawa Shuppansha.

Kim, Mungil (2003), *Tsuda Sen to chosen: Chosen kirisuto-kyo juyo to sin-nogyo seisaku* [Tsuda Sen and Korea: Acceptance of Korean Christianity and New Agricultural Policy], Kyoto: Sekai Shisosha.

Kimura, Keiko (2002), *Kawai Michi no shogai: Hikari ni ayunda hito* [The Life of Kawai Michi: The Person Who Walked in the Light], Tokyo: Iwanami Shoten.

Kira, Yoshie (ed.) (2021), *Naruse Jinzo to Nihon Joshi Daigakko no jidai* [The Age of Naruse Jinzo and Japan Women's University], Tokyo: Nippon Keizai Hyoronsha.

Kodate, Naonori and Kashiko Kodate (2016), *Japanese Women in Science and Engineering: History and Policy Change*, London and New York: Routledge.

Kodate, Naonori and Kashiko Kodate (2022), "Career Path Dependent and Supported: The Role of Women's Universities in Ensuring Access to STEM Education and Research Careers in Japan," in Clare G. Jones, Alison E. Martin, and Alexis Wolf (eds.), *The Palgrave Handbook of Women and Science since 1660*, London: Palgrave Macmillan, pp. 195–222

Kohler, Robert E. (1990), "The Ph.D. Machines: Building on the Collegiate Base." *Isis*, vol. 81, pp. 638–662.

Kohler, Robert E. (1994), *Lords of the Fly:* Drosophila *Genetics and the Experimental Life*, Chicago and London: University of Chicago Press.

Koizumi, Koichi (2008), "Sanga haruka: Joshu senjin no kiseki: 5: Hoshino Ai, 1–10 [The Search: Predecessors' Trails in Joshu 5: Hoshino Ai, 1–10]," *Jomo Shimbun*, July 15–19, 21–25, August 5.

Komai, Taku (1947), *Dahwin no ie* [Darwin's House], Tokyo: Sogensha.

Komai, Taku (1967), "T. H. Morgan's Times: A Japanese Scientist Reminisces," *The Journal of Heredity*, vol. 58, no. 5 (September–October), pp. 247–250.

Koyama, Shizuko (2013), *Ryosai Kenbo: The Educational Ideal of 'Good Wife, Wise Mother' in Modern Japan*, trans. by Stephen Filler, Boston: Brill.

Kuniyoshi, Sakae (2018), *Mori Arinori ga kirihiraita nichibei gaiko: Shadai chubei gaiko-kan no chosen* [The U.S.-Japan Diplomacy that Mori Arinori Opened: The Challenge of the First Diplomat to the United States], Tokyo: Bensei Shuppan.

Kuno, Akiko (1993a), *Rokumeikan no kifujin: Oyama Sutematsu, nihon hatsu no joshi ryugaku-sei* [The Lady of Rokumeikan: Oyama Sutematsu, the First Japanese Woman to Study Abroad], Tokyo: Chuko bunko.

Kuno, Akiko (1993b), *Unexpected Destinations: The Poignant Story of Japan's First Vassar Graduate*, trans. (of Kuno (1993a)) by Kirsten McIvor, Tokyo: Kodansha International.

Kuroda, Kotaro (2019), "Kuroda Chika no shogai: Josei kagakusha no sakigake no kiseki [The Life of Kuroda Chika: The Trajectory of a Pioneering Female Chemist]," in Kagakushi Gakkai (Japanese Society for the History of Chemistry) (ed.), *Kagakushi eno shotai* [Invitation to the History of Chemistry], Tokyo: Ohmsha, pp. 178–188.

Kuroiwa, Hisako (2008), *Meiji no ojosama* [Ladies in the Meiji Era], Tokyo: Kadokawa Sensho.

Kusano, Atsuko T. and Karolyn Sewell (1993), "The Japanese University Accreditation Association and Dr. Lulu Holmes—1946–1948: One Historical Aspect on the Founding of New Universities for Women in Japan after World War II," *Journal of Home Economics of Japan*, vol. 44, no. 3, pp. 173–184.

Kuwaki, Ayao (1941), "Kagakushi no kenkyu [Study of the History of Science]," *Kagakusi Kenkyu* (Journal of History of Science, Japan), no. 1, pp. 2–10.

Lillie, Frank R. (1944), *The Woods Hole Marine Biological Laboratory*, Chicago: University of Chicago Press.

Maeda, Koko (1995), "Kuroda Chika: Tennen shikiso kenkyu ni okeru gyoseki to wagakuni hatsuno josei kagakusha toshiteno shogai [Kuroda Chika: Her Achievements in Natural Pigment Research and Her Life as Japan's First Female Chemist]," *Kagakushi* (Journal for the Japanese Society for the History of Chemistry), no. 22, pp. 226–238.

Maeda, Koko (2004), "Kato Sechi hakase no kenkyu to shogai: Supekutoru no butsuri-kagaku teki kaimei wo mezashite [The Research and Life of Dr. Kato Sechi: Toward the Physico-chemical Elucidation of Spectra]," *Jendaa Kenkyu* (Gender Studies), no. 7, pp. 87–110.

Maienschein, Jane (1991). *Transforming Traditions in American Biology, 1880–1915*, Baltimore and London: Johns Hopkins University Press.

Mamatkulova, Nilfar (2011a), "Shoki no Joshi Eigaku Juku ni okeru kyojuho ni kansuru ichi kosatsu: Tsuda Umeko no mezashita koto kyoiku [A Study of Teaching Methods in Early Women's English Schools: Tsuda Umeko's Aim for Higher Education]," *Waseda Daigaku Kyoiku Gakkai Kiyo* (Bulletin of the Educational Society of Waseda University), no. 12, pp. 79–86.

Mamatkulova, Nilfar (2011b), "Joshi Eigaku Juku ni okeru kyoiku jissen no seika ni kansuru ichi kosatsu: Tsuda Umeko no nerai to shoki sotsugyo-sei no shinro [A Study on the Results of Educational Practices at Joshi Eigaku Juku: Tsuda Umeko's Aim and the Career Paths of the Early Graduates]," *Waseda Kyoiku Hyoron* (Waseda Review of Education), vol. 25, no. 1, pp. 107–125.

Mamatkulova, Nilfar (2021), "Tsuda Umeko no nihon josei-zo: Joshi Eigaku Juku sosetsu no haikei wo meguru kensho [Japanese Female Image of Tsuda Umeko: An Examination of the Background to the Founding of Joshi Eigaku Juku]," *Ajia Kyoikushi Kenkyu* (Research of Educational History in Asia), vol. 30, pp. 27–41.

Meigs, Cornelia (1956), *What Makes a College? A History of Bryn Mawr*, New York: The Macmillan Company.

Miki, Hisako (2004), "Yasui Kono no shogai [The Life of Yasui Kono]," *Yasui Kono shiryo mokuroku* [Catalogue of Materials of Yasui Kono], Tokyo: Ochanomizu Joshi Daigaku jenda kenkyu sentaa (Ochanomizu University Institute for Gender Studies), pp. 6–113.

Mitsukuri, Kakichi (1898), "Dobutsugaku no ichi shin bunka [A New Division of Zoology]," *Toyo Gakugei Zasshi*, no. 207, pp. 519–521.

Miyake, K. and K. Yasui (1911), "On the gametophytes and Embryo of *Pseudolarix,*" *Annals of Botany*, vol. 25, pp. 639–647.

Miyakoda, Toyosaburo (2000), *Tsuda Sen: Meiji no kirisuto-sha* [Tsuda Sen: The Christian of the Meiji Era], Tokyo: Ozora-sha.

Miyata, Yukie (1993), "Yasui Tetsu no joshi koto kyoiku-ron [Yasui Tetsu's Views of Women's Higher Education]," *Kyoiku Kagaku Kenkyu* (Journal of Scientific Research on Education, Shuto Daigaku Tokyo (Tokyo Metropolitan University)), no. 12, pp. 1–9.

Miyazaki, Akane (2013), "Suzuki Hideru: Josei yakugaku hakase dai ichi go [Suzuki Hideru: The First Female Doctor of Pharmacy]," in Nihon Joshi Daigaku rigaku kyoiku kenkyukai (ed.) 2013, pp. 99–124.

Miyoshi, Manabu (1938), *Gakuken-shu: zuihitsu* [Gakuken Collected Essays], Tokyo: Iwanami Shoten.

Mizoguchi, Hajime (1981), "Amerika hassei-gaku seiritu no ichi sokumen: 'Saibo keito' kenkyu wo chusin ni [An Aspect of the Establishment of American Embryology: Focusing on the Study of 'Cell Lineage']," *Seibutsugakushi Kenkyu* (The Japanese Journal of the History of Biology), vol. 8, no. 1, pp. 11–12.

Mizoguchi, Hajime (1999), "Dobutsu gakusha Mitsukuri Kakichi, Yatsu Naohide no Taibei zaigaku kiroku ni tsuite [On the Record of the Zoologists Mitsukuri Kakichi and Yatsu Naohide's Stay in America]," *Seibutsugakushi Kenkyu* (The Japanese Journal of the History of Biology), no. 64, pp. 65–75

Mizoguchi, Hajime (2001a), "Nihon no seio kindai dobutsugaku no jiritsu to jonzu hopukinsu daigaku zaisekisha [Independence of Western Modern Zoology in Japan and Students at Johns Hopkins University]," *Seibutsugakushi Kenkyu* (The Japanese Journal of the History of Biology), no. 68, pp. 1–13.

Mizoguchi, Hajime (2001b), "Uzzu horu rinkai jikkenjo ni okeru nihonjin kenkyusha no katsudo [Activities of Japanese Researchers at the Woods Hole Marine Biological Laboratory]," *Z News,* May, pp. 16–20.

Mizoguchi, Hajime (2002), "Rinkai jikkenjo to hasseigaku: Mitsugetsu to kairi, sosite aratana mosaku [Marine Biological Laboratories and Embryology: From Honeymoon to Divergence, and New Search]," *Seibutsu Kagaku* (Biological Sciences), vol. 54, no. 1, pp. 40–50.

Mizoguchi, Hajime (2005), "Noguchi Hideyo to uzzu hori rinaki jikkennjo: kanegi kenkyuusho niyoru josei tono kankeikara [Noguchi Hideyo and the Woods Hole Marine Biological Laboratory: In Relation to the Grant by the Carnegie Institution]," *Seibutsugakushi Kenkyu* (The Japanese Journal of the History of Biology), no. 74, pp. 7–26.

Monbu-sho (Ministry of Education) (ed.) (1972), *Gakusei 100 nenshi, shiryo hen* [One Hundred Year History of the School System, Document Volume], Tokyo: Monbu-sho.

Morgan, Thomas Hunt and Umé Tsuda (1894), "The Orientation of the Frog's Egg," *Quarterly Journal of Microscopical Science*, vol. 35, pp. 373–405.

Morgan, Thomas Hunt (1897), *The Development of the Frog's Egg: An Introduction to Experimental Embryology*, London: Macmillan Company.

Morgan, Thomas Hunt (1940), "Edmund Beecher Wilson, 1856–1939," *National Academy of Sciences Biographical Memoirs*, vol. XXI, pp. 315–342.

Morris-Suzuki, Tessa (1995), "The Great Translation: Traditional and Modern Science in Japan's Industrialisation," *Historia Scientiarum*, vol. 5, no. 2, pp. 103–16.

Mukogawa Josidaigaku Kyoiku Sogo Kenkyusho (Mukogawa Women's University Institute of Education) (2025), "Joshi daigaku tokei [Statistics on Women's Colleges and Universities]," https://kyoken.mukogawa-u.ac.jp/statistics/, accessed October 1, 2025.

Muller, H. J. (1943), "Edmund B. Wilson—An Appreciation," *The American Naturalist*, vol. LXXVII, pp. 5–37 and 142–172.

Murata, Suzuko (1980), *Wagakuni joshi koto kyoiku seiritsu katei no kenkyu* [A Study of the Process of Establishing Women's Higher Education in Japan], Tokyo: Kazama Shobo.

Nagashima, Yuzuru (1937), *Onna hakase retsuden* [Biographies of Women Doctors], Tokyo: Meiji Shoin.

Nagatoya, Yoji (1958), "Okami Keiko: Joshi ryugaku-sei dai ichigo [Okami Keiko: the First International Female Medical Student," *Nippon Ijishinpou* (Japan Medical Journal), no. 1807, pp. 49–54.

Naimu-sho Eisei-kyoku (Ministry of Home Affairs, Public Health Bureau) (ed.) (2008), *Ryukosei kanbo "supein kaze" dairyuko no kiroku* [Record of the Great Epidemic of the Epidemic Cold "Spanish Flu"], Tokyo: Heibonsha.

Nakahara, Lisa and Ariga Nobuyuki (2019), "Josei Butsuri-gakusha no shushin-ko toshiteno Tokyo Joshi Koto Shihan Gakko: Otobe Kokichi no butsurigaku kyoiku ni chakumoku shite [Tokyo Women's Higher Normal School as a School Where Female Physicists Emerged: Focusing on the Physics Education of Otobe Kokichi]," *Kokuritsu Kagaku Hakubutsukan Kenkyu Hokoku* (National Museum of Nature and Science Research Report), E (Science and Engineering), vol. 42, pp. 11–24.

Nakamura, Setsuko (2007), "Eiyo to karada no kankei no Kenkyu de yononaka ni yakudachitai: Tange Ume [I Want to Help the World by Studying the Relationship between Nutrition and the Body: Tange Ume], in Iwao and Hara (eds.) 2007, pp. 8–15

Nakamura, Chiyomatsu (1906), *Jicchi seisa joshi yugaku binran* [On-site Inspection, Guidebook for Girls' Study Tour], Tokyo: Joshi Bundansha.

Nakanishi, Fumiko (1929), "Tsuda-sensei no koto [Something about Tsuda-Sensei]," *Eigo Seinen* (The Rising Generation), vol. 62, no. 3, pp. 102–103.

Nakazawa, Shingo (1988), "Dobutsu gakusha Tsuda Umeko [Zoologist Tsuda Umeko]," *Iden* (Genetics), vol. 42, no. 8, pp. 46–49.

Namimatsu, Nobuhisa (2013), "Meijiki ni okeru Tsuda Sen no keimo katsudo: Oubei nogyo no fukyu to kirisuto-kyo no yakuwari [Tsuda Sen's Enlightenment Activities in the Meiji Period: The Diffusion of Western Agriculture and the Role of Christianity]" *Kyoto Sangyo Daigaku Ronshu* (Kyoto Sangyo University Departmental Bulletin Papers, Social Science), vol. 30, pp. 85–122.

National Diet Library Research (1943), "Kyoiku ni kansuru senjiki hijo sochi hosaku [Emergency Wartime Measures Concerning Education]," October 21, National Diet Library Research Navi: https://rnavi.ndl.go.jp/politics/entry/bib00512.php, accessed October 1, 2025.

Nihon Joshi Daigakko (Japan Women's University) (ed.) (1942), *Nihon Joshi Daigakko 40 nenshi* [Forty Year History of Japan Women's University], Tokyo: Nihon Joshi Daigakko.

Nihon Joshi Daigaku (Japan Women's University) (ed.) (2001), *Nihon Joshi Daigaku Gakuen Jiten: Soritsu 100 nen no kiseki* [Dictionary of Japan Women's University: Trajectory of 100 years since its Foundation], Tokyo: Domes Shuppan.

Nihon Joshi Daigaku rigaku kyoiku kenkyukai (Japan Women's University Science Education Study Group) (ed.) (2013), *Joshi rigaku kyoiku wo riido shita josei kagakusha tachi: Reimeiki, Meiji kohan kara no kiseki* [Women Scientists Who Led Women's Science Education: Trajectories from the Dawn of the Age and the Latter Half of the Meiji Era], Tokyo: Akashi Shoten.

Nimura, Janice P. (2015), *Daughters of the Samurai: A Journey from East to West and Back*, New York and London: W. W. Norton.

Nukada, Yutaka (1942), "Rigaku senmon gakko setsuritsu shushi no ittan [A Part of the Purpose of the Establishment of the Science School]," *Koho* (Magazine of Imperial Women's Medical and Pharmaceutical College), vol. 10, pp. 4–5.

Oba, Minako (1990), *Tsuda Umeko*, Tokyo: Asahi Shimbun-sha.

Oba, Minako (2021), *Reflections on Tsuda Umeko: Pioneer of Women's Education in Japan*, trans. (of Oba (1990)) by Tani Yu, Tokyo: Japan Publishing Industry Foundation for Culture.

Ogawa, Mariko (2017), "History of Women's Participation in STEM Fields in Japan," *Asian Women*, vol. 33, no. 3, pp. 65–85.

Ohashi, Hiro (1974), *Ohashi Hiro iko-shu* [Ohashi Hiro's Posthumous Manuscripts], ed. by Ohashi Hiro iko hensankai (Ohashi Hiro's Posthumous Manuscripts Compilation Committee), Tokyo: Ohashi Hiro iko hensankai.

Okada, Daishi (2009), "Kokunaigai no kenkyu jokyo no henka ga wagakuni ni okeru kenkyusha shudan no keisei ni ataeta eikyo: 'Nihon Rigakushi Gakkai' to 'Nihon Kagakushi Gakkai' no tachiagari ni kanyo shita shudan wo hikaku shite [The Influence of Changes in Research Conditions at Home and Abroad on the Formation of the Group of Researchers in Japan: A Comparison of the groups involved in the formation of 'Nihon Rigakushi Gakkai' and 'Nihon Kagakushi Gakkai']," *Kagakusi Kenkyu* (Journal of History of Science, Japan), vol. 58, no. 291, pp. 264–274.

Oppenheimer, Jane M. (1967), *Essays in the History of Embryology and Biology*, Cambridge, Massachusetts: The MIT Press.

Oppenheimer, Jane M. (1983), "Thomas Hunt Morgan as an Embryologist: The View from Bryn Mawr," *American Zoologist*, vol. 23, pp. 845–854.

Oshima, Hiroshi (1950), *Ichi dobutsu gakusha no kiroku: Ikoku wo urotsuku* [Record of a Zoologist: Wandering around Foreign Countries], Tokyo: Kantosha.

Pauly, Philip J. (1984), "The Appearance of Academic Biology in Late Nineteenth Century America," *Journal of the History of Biology*, vol. 17, no. 3, pp. 367–397.

Pauly, Philip J. (1987), *Controlling Life: Jacques Loeb and The Engineering Ideal in Biology*, New York and Oxford: Oxford University Press.

Pauly, Philip J. (1988), "Summer Resort and Scientific Discipline: Woods Hole and the Structure of American Biology, 1882–1925," in Rainger et al. (eds.) 1988, pp. 121–150.

Rainger, Ronald, Keith R. Benson, and Jane Maienschein (eds.) (1988), *The American Development of Biology*, New Brunswick and London: Rutgers University Press.

Rikagaku Kenkyusho 100 nenshi henshu iinkai (RIKEN Centennial History Editorial Board) (ed.) (2018), *Rikagaku Kenkyusho 100 nenshi* [RIKEN Centennial History], Wako: Rikagaku Kenkyusho.

Rose, Barbara (1992), *Tsuda Umeko and Women's Education in Japan*, New Haven: Yale University Press.

Rossiter, Margaret W. (1982), *Women Scientists in America: Struggles and Strategies*, Baltimore: Johns Hopkins University Press.

Saijo, Toshimi (2009), *Rikei no tobira wo hiraita nihon no josei tachi: Yukari no chi wo tazunete* [Japanese Women Who Opened the Doors to Science: Visiting the Places Associated with Them], Tokyo: Shinsensha.

Saito, Yukio (1968), *Nihon nogakushi: Kindai nogaku keiseiki no kenkyu* [History of Agronomy in Japan: A Study of the Formative Period of Modern Agricultural Science], Tokyo: Nogyo Sogo-kenkyusho.

Sakamoto, Tatsuro (2000), "Tsuda Umeko to josei no koto kyoiku daiichi sedai tachi: 19-seiki matsu no amerika gashu-koku ni okeru josei no koto kyoiku sien undo [Tsuda Umeko and the First Generation of Women in Higher Education: Women's Higher Education Support Movement in the United States at the End of the 19th Century]," in Iino et al. (eds.) 2000, pp. 27–47.

Sakurai, Mamoru (1943), *Joshi Kyoikushi* [History of Women's Education], Tokyo: Seishindo.

Sano, Mayuko (2019), *Kurara Hoittonii ga tsuzutta meiji no hibi* [Clara Whitney's Meiji Days], Kyoto: Rinsen Shoten.

Sasaki, Keiko (2002), *Senzenki joshi koto kyoiku no ryoteki kakudai katei: Seifu, seito, gakko no dainamizumu* [The Quantitative Expansion Process of Women's Higher Education in the Prewar Period: Dynamics of Government, Students, and Schools], Tokyo: Tokyo Daigaku Shuppankai.

Sawayanagi, Masataro (1924), "Oubei no joshi kyoiku [Girls' Education in Europe and America]," in Kokumin Kyoiku Shoreikai (Committee for Promotion of People's Education) (ed.), *Gendai bunka to kyoiku* [Modern Culture and Education], Tokyo: Minyusha, pp. 286–317.

Sedgwick, William T. and Edmund B. Wilson (1886), *General Biology*, New York: Henry Holt.

Senju, Katsumi (1967), "Meiji-ki joshi-kyoiku no sho-mondai: kan-ko-ritu wo chusin tosite [Various Issues in Meiji Women's Education: Focusing on Governmental and Public Education]," Nihon Joshi Daigaku Joshi Kyoiku Kenkyusho (Institute for Research in Women's Education, Japan Women's University) (ed.), *Meiji no joshi kyoiku* (Women's Education in the Meiji Era), Tokyo: Kokudosha, pp. 8–41.

Serizawa, Yumi and Toda Tetsuko (2002), "Ikyo eno kikoku: Tsuda Umeko shokan ni miru nihon [Returning to a Foreign Country: Japan in Tsuda Umeko's Letters]," *Yamanashi Ken-ritsu Joshi Tandai Chiho Kenkyu* (Yamanashi Women's Junior College Regional Studies), no. 2, pp. 103–117.

Shapiro, Laura (2009), *Perfection Salad: Women and Cooking at the Turn of the Century*, Berkeley and Los Angeles: University of California Press.

Shimizu, Takako (2001), "Tsuda Umeko no *The Attic Letters* ni miru ibunka hen-yo [The Cross-Cultural Transformation in Tsuda Umeko's *The Attic Letters*]," *Nippon Bunri Daigaku Kiyo* (Bulletin of Nippon Bunri University), vol. 29, no. 2, pp. 95–106.

Shine, Ian and Sylvia Wrobel (1976), *Thomas Hunt Morgan: Pioneer of Genetics*, Lexington: University Press of Kentucky.

Shirai, Takako (2018), *Meiji-ki joshi kyoiku ni okeru nichi-ei no koryu: Tsuda Umeko, Naruse Jinzo, Hyuzu, Firippus wo megutte* [Anglo-Japanese Exchange in Girls' Higher Education during the Meiji Period: With Regard to Tsuda Umeko, Naruse Jinzo, Hughes, and Phillips], Tokyo: Domesu Shuppan.

Sturtevant, A. H. (1959), "Thomas Hunt Morgan, September 25, 1866–December 4, 1945," *National Academy of Sciences Biographical Memoirs*, vol. XXXIII, pp. 282–325.

Sueki, Setsuko (2001), "Tsuda Umeko's byoki kan [Tsuda Umeko's View of Illness]," *Sogo Kango* (Comprehensive Nursing), vol. 36, no. 2, pp. 51–57.

T., U. [Tsuda, Ume] (1904), "Hon. Sen Tsuda," *The Japan Evangelist*, vol. XI, no. 9 (September), pp. 273–275.

Takahashi, Yuko (2000), "Alice Bacon to Oyama Sutematsu: Umeko wo sien sita Bacon-ke no 'musume-tachi' [Alice Bacon and Oyama Sutematsu: The Bacon Family's 'Daughters' Who Supported Umeko]," in Iino et al. (eds.) 2000, pp. 49–70.

Takahashi, Yuko (2002), *Tsuda Umeko no shakai-shi* [A Social History of Tsuda Umeko], Tokyo: Tamagawa Daigaku Shuppanbu.

Takahashi, Yuko (2013), "Shoken kotaigo to Tsuda Umeko: Kazoku Jogakko deno setten wo chusin ni [Empress Dowager Shoken and Tsuda Umeko: Focusing on Their Contacts at the Peeresses' School]," *Meiji Seitoku Kinen Gakkai Kiyo* (Transactions of the Meiji Japan Society), no. 50, pp. 635–644.

Takahashi, Yuko (2022), *Tsuda Umeko: Joshi kyoiku wo hiraku* [Tsuda Umeko: Opening up a Path to Women's Education], Tokyo: Iwanami Shoten.

Takamine Hideo-sensei kinen jigyo kai (Takamine Hideo Memorial Project Association) (ed.) (1987), *Takamine Hideo-sensei den* [Biography of Takamine Hideo sensei], Tokyo: Oozorasha.

Takasaki, Soji (2008), *Tsuda Sen hoyden; Mo hitotsu no kindaika wo mezashita hito* [Biography of Tsuda Sen: A Man Who Aimed for Another Modernization], Urayasu: Sofukan.

Takemata, Hatsumi (1990), "Kaseigaku undo to josei no katei-teki yakuwari: Amerika josei-shi no shiten kara [The Home Economic Movement and Women's Domestic Roles: From the Perspective of American Women's History]," *Amerika Kenkyu* (American Studies), no. 24, pp. 143–162.

Tamaki, Tamotsu (1998), *Dobutsu gakusha Mitsukuri Kakichi to sono jidai: Meiji jin wa nani wo kangaetaka* [Zoologist Mitsukuri Kakichi and His Time: What Did the Meiji People Think?], Tokyo: San-ichi Shobo.

Tanioka, Ikuko (1998), "Kindai joshi koto-kyoiku kikan no seiritsu to gakko dezain [Establishment of Modern Women's Higher Education Institutions and School Design]," Kobe Geijutsu Koka Daigaku (Kobe Design University), doctoral dissertation.

Terasaka, Yumi (2001), "Meiji joshi ryugaku-sei no nyushin ni kansuru ichi kosatu: Tsuda Umeko no baai [A Discussion on the Initiation of Meiji Women Students into Christianity: The Case of Tsuda Umeko]," *Taisho Daigaku Daigakuin Kenkyu Ronshu* (Journal of the Graduate School, Taisho University), no. 25, pp. 278–265.

The Marine Biological Laboratory (1891), *The Marine Biological Laboratory Fourth Annual Report for the Year 1891*, Boston: The Marine Biological Laboratory.

Toho Daigaku Rigakubu 50 shunen kinen jigyo iinkai (Toho University Faculty of Science 50th Anniversary Commemorative Project Committee) (ed.) (1991), *Toho Daigaku Rigakubu 50 shunen-shi* [50-Year History of Toho University Faculty of Science], Tokyo: Toho Daigaku Rigakubu 50 shunen Kinen Jigyo Iinkai.

Tokyo Joshi Koto Shihan Gakko (Tokyo Women's Higher Normal School) (ed.) (1898–1900), *Tokyo Joshi Koto Shihan Gakko ichiran* [Overview of Tokyo Women's Higher Normal Schools], Tokyo: Tokyo Joshi Koto Shihan Gakko.

Tokyo Joshi Koto Shihan Gakko (Tokyo Women's Higher Normal School) (ed.) (1934), *Tokyo Joshi Koto Shihan Gakko rokuju nenshi* [Sixty-Year History of Tokyo Women's Higher Normal School], Tokyo: Tokyo Joshi Koto Shihan Gakko.

Tokyo-to (Tokyo Metropolitan Government) (ed.) (1969), *Nihon no joshi daigaku* [Women's Universities in Japan], Tokyo: Tokyo-to.

Tsuda Eigaku Juku (ed.) (1941), *Tsuda Eigaku Juku 40 nenshi* [Forty Years of Tsuda Eigaku Juku], Tokyo: Tsuda Eigaku Juku.

Tsuda Eigaku Juku no shorai no jigyo hoshin ni kansuru shingi iinkai (Deliberative Committee on the Future Administration Policy of Tsuda Eigaku Juku) (1942), "Toshinsho [Report]," cited in Hoshino 1943, pp. 3–5.

Tsuda Juku Daigaku (ed.) (1960), *Tsuda Juku 60 nenshi* [Sixty Years of Tsuda Juku], Tokyo: Tsuda Juku Daigaku.

Tsuda Juku Daigaku (ed.) (1984), *Tsuda Umeko bunsho* [The Writings of Tsuda Umeko], revised edition, Tokyo: Tsuda Juku Daigaku.

Tsuda Juku Daigaku 100 nenshi hensan iinkai (Tsuda College 100 Year History Compilation Committee) (ed.) (2003), *Tsuda Juku Daigaku 100 nenshi* [100th Anniversary of Tsuda College], 2 vols., Tokyo: Tsuda Juku Daigaku.

Tsuda Juku Daigaku soritsu 90 shunen kinen jigyo shuppan iinkai (Tsuda College 90th Anniversary Memorial Publication Committee) (ed.) (1990), *Tsuda Juku Daigaku: Tsuda Umeko to Juku no 90 nen* [Tsuda University: Tsuda Umeko and the School's 90 Years], Tokyo: Tsuda Juku Daigaku.

Tsuda Juku Daigaku soritsu 100 shunen kinen-shi shuppan iinkai (Publication Committee for the 100th Anniversary of Tsuda College) (ed.) (2000), *Michi eno yuuki: Uke tugareru Tsuda supiritto* [Courage to the Unknown: The Inherited Tsuda Spirit], Tokyo: Tsuda Juku Dosokai.

Tsuda Juku Rika no rekishi wo kiroku suru kai (Group for Recording the History of the Tsuda Juku Science Department) (ed.) (1987), *Josei no jiritsu to kagaku kyoiku: Tsuda Juku rika no rekishi* [Women's Independence and Science Education: History of Tsuda Juku Science Department], Tokyo: Domesu Shuppan.

Tsuda, Michio (2012), *Tsuda Sen no shinzoku tachi* [Tsuda Sen's Relatives], Tokyo: Miyaobi Publishing.

Tsuda, Noboru (ed.) (1958), *Tsuda Sen'oo ryaku-den* [Brief Biography of Old Mr. Tsuda Sen], Private publication.

Tsuda, Sen (1874), *Huiburen-shi ho nogyo sanji* [Mr. Hooibrenk's Three Processes in Agriculture], Tokyo: Maekawa Zenbei and Aoyama Seikichi.

Tsuda, Sen (1875), "Kaka baijoho no setsu [Theory of Pollination of Rice Flowers]," *Meiroku Zasshi*, no. 41, reprinted in Yamamuro Shinichi and Nakanome Toru (eds.), *Meiroku Zasshi*, vol. 3, Tokyo: Iwanami bunko (2009), pp. 326–334.

Tsuda, Sen (1897), "Okoku hakurankai nogyo engei no denshu oyobi sono go no jokyo [The Situation of Learning of Agriculture and Horticulture at the World Exposition in Austria and its Aftermath]" in Tanaka Yoshio and Hirayama Narinobu (eds.), *Okoku hakurankai sando kiyo* [The Bulletin of Participation in the Austrian Exposition], vol. 3, Tokyo: Moriyama Haruo, pp. 33–36.

Tsuda, Ume (1891), "The Education of Japanese Women," August 2, 1891, reproduced in Tsuda Juku Daigaku (ed.) 1984, pp. 28–33.

Tsuda, Ume (1991), *The Attic Letters: Ume Tsuda's Correspondence to Her American Mother*, ed. by Furuki Yoshiko, editor-in-chief, New York and Tokyo: Weatherhill.

Tsuda, Umeko (1895), "Kaji kyoiku no hitsuyo [The Necessity of Domestic Education]," *Nihon no Katei* (Japanese Home), December 1895, reproduced in Tsuda Juku Daigaku (ed.) 1984, pp. 23–25.

Tsuda, Umeko (1900), "Resume of a talk given by Miss Tsuda, head of the Joshi Ei-Gaku-Juku at the opening of the school work, Sept. 14th, 1900," reproduced in *Tsuda Juku Daigaku 100 nenshi*, vol.1, pp. 67–70; The Japanese translation: "Kaiko shikiji [Address at the Opening Ceremony]," reproduced in Tsuda Juku Daigaku (ed.) 1984, p. 1–4.

Tsuda, Umeko (1908), "Yomi fuketta denki [The Biographies I Was Absorbed in Reading]," *Shojo Sekai* (The World of Girls), August, reprinted in Tsuda Juku Daigaku (ed.)1984, p. 68.

Tsugawa, Akiko (2004), "Kagaku to jendaa [Science and Gender]," *Tokyo Ikashika Daigaku Kyoyo-bu Kenkyu Kiyo* (Bulletin of the Faculty of Liberal Arts, Tokyo Medical and Dental University), no. 34, pp. 95–108.

Tsugawa, Akiko and Kanomi Satoko (1996), *Hiraku: Nihon no josei kagakusha no kiseki* [Opening: The Trajectories of Japanese Women Scientists], Tokyo: Domesu Shuppan.

Tsuji, Kiyo (ed.) (1953), *Senkakusha Tange-sensei* [The Pioneer Tange-sensei]," Tokyo: Nihon Joshi Daigaku Kosetsu Kagaku-kan.

Uchida, Michiko (2000), "Meari H. Morisu shogaku-kin: Nihon no josei ni Umeko to onaji kikai wo [Mary H. Morris Scholarship: For the Same Opportunity for Japanese Women as Umeko]," in Iino et al. (eds.) 2000, pp. 177–201.

Ueda, Akiko (2000), "Hoshino Ai: Arashi no naka no 30 nen [Hoshino Ai: 30 Years in the Storm]," in Iino et. al (eds.) 2000, pp. 259–278.

Ueda, Hisashi (1986), *Nishida Kitaro no tsum*a [Nishida Kitaro's Wife], Tokyo: Nansosha.

Uemura, Chikako (2007), *Josei kaiho wo meguru senryo seisaku* [Occupation Policy Regarding Women's Liberation], Tokyo: Keiso Shobo.

Ueno, Kayuki; Sato Kimiko; and Matsuda Hisako (2000), "Hoshino Ai: Tsuda Juku sonbo no kiki wo sukutta hito—rika zosetu ketudan [Hoshino Ai: The Person Who Rescued Tsuda Juku's Existence—The Decision to Create the Science Department]," in Tsuda Juku Daigaku soritsu 100 shunen kinen-shi shuppan iinkai (ed.) 2000, pp. 19–21.

United States Education Mission (1946), "Beikoku shisetsu-dan hokoku-sho (yoshi) [Report of the U.S. Mission (Summary)] (1946)," (March 31, 1946) in Monbu-sho (ed.) 1972, pp. 58–61.

Waller, John (2017), *Heredity: A Very Short Introduction*, Oxford: Oxford University Press.

Watanabe, Masao (1976a), *Nihon-jin to Kindai Kagaku* [Japanese and Modern Science], Tokyo: Iwanami Shinsho.

Watanabe, Masao (1976b), *Oyatoi Amerika-jin kagaku kyoshi* (Hired American Science Teachers), Tokyo: Kodansha.

Watanabe, Masao (1990), *The Japanese and Western Science*, trans. (of Watanabe Masao (1976a)) by Otto Theodor Benfey, Philadelphia: University of Pennsylvania Press.

Watanabe, Yoko (2014), *Kindai nihon no josei senmon-shoku kyoiku: Shogai kyoikugaku kara mita Tokyo Joshi Ika Daigaku soritsu sha Yoshioka Yayoi* [Women's Professional Education in Modern Japan: Yayoi Yoshioka, Founder of Tokyo Women's Medical University from the Viewpoint of Lifelong Education], Tokyo: Akashi Shoten.

Whitney, Clara (1885), *Tegaru seiyo ryori* [Easy Western Cooking], trans. by Tsuda Sen and Sarashiro Kin, Tokyo: Eto Shoten.

Whitney, Clara (1996), *Clara no meiji nikki: Katsu Kaishu no yome* [Clara's Meiji Diary: Katsu Kaishu's Daughter-in-law], trans. by Ichimata Tamiko et al., 2 vols., Tokyo: Chuko Bunko.

Yajima, Suketoshi (1949), "Kuwaki Ayao no tsuioku: Sono gyoseki to gakufu [Reminiscences of Kuwaki Ayao: His Achievements and Academic Style]," *Kagakusi Kenkyu* (Journal of History of Science, Japan), no. 10, pp. 19–22.

Yamada, Yuka (2024), "Tokyo Joshi Koto Shihan Gakko no rika kyoiku ga josei seibutsugakusha ni ataeta eikyo: Iwakawa Tomotaro no seibutsugaku kyoiku ni chakumoku shite [The Impact of Science Education at Tokyo Women's Higher Normal School on Female Biologists: Focusing on Biology Education Provided by Iwakawa Tomotaro]," *Seibutsu Shigen Kagaku* (Bioresource Sciences, Nihon Uiversity), vol. 33, pp. 15–24.

Yamakawa, Kenjiro (1911), "Nihon jinshu to joshi no kenko [The Japanese Race and Women's Health]," in *Shin Katei* (New Home), March, reproduced in Yamakawa Kenjiro 1937, pp. 732–735.

Yamakawa, Kenjiro (1937), *Danshaku Yamakawa-sensei iko* [Baron

Yamakawa-Sensei's Posthumous Manuscripts] ed. by Ko-Yamakawa Danshaku Kinen-kai (Late Baron Yamakawa Memorial Association), Tokyo: Ko-Yamakawa Danshaku Kinen-kai.

Yamakawa, Kikue (1929), "Eigaku kai no sentaku-sha Tsuda-sensei [Tsuda-sensei, The Pioneer in the Field of English Studies]," *Fujin Koron* (October, 1929), reproduced in Yamakawa Kikue 1982b, pp. 169–178.

Yamakawa, Kikue (1972), *Onna nidai no ki* [An Essay on Two Generations of Women], Tokyo: Heibonsha.

Yamakawa, Kikue (1982a), *Yamakawa Kikue shu* [Collected Essays of Yamakawa Kikue], ed. by Tanaka Sumiko and Yamakawa Shinsaku, 4: *Musan kaikyu no fujin undo* [Women's Movement of the Proletariat], Tokyo: Iwanami Shoten.

Yamakawa, Kikue (1982b), *Yamakawa Kikue shu* [Collected Essays of Yamakawa Kikue], ed. by Tanaka Sumiko and Yamakawa Shinsaku, 8: *Kono hitobito* [These People], Tokyo: Iwanami Shoten.

Yamamoto, Mihoko (2006), "1920 nen 'Gakuirei'-ka ni okeru josei no gakui shutoku jokyo [The Acquisition of Degrees by Women under the 1920 'Degree Order'], *Hokkaido Daigaku Daigaku-bunshokan Nenpo* (Annual Report of Hokkaido University Archives), no. 11, pp. 59–73.

Yamamoto, Mihoko (2008), "1918–1945 nen ni okeru teikokudaigaku daigakuin eno josei no shingaku jokyo (1) : Kagaku senko no shingakusha ni chakumoku shite [Women's Entrance to Graduate Schools of Imperial Universities in 1918–1945 (1): Focusing on those Who Majored in Chemistry]," *Hokkaido Daigaku Daigaku Bunsho-kan Nenpo* (Annual Report of Hokkaido University Archives), no. 13, pp. 48–61.

Yamamoto, Mihoko (2017), "'Kagaku wa josei ni totte nanimono nimo masaru bifuku dearu': Josei kagakusha nosenkusha Kato Sechi no ayumi ['Science is a beautiful garment superior to anything else for women': The Trajectory of the Pioneer Women Scientist Kato Sechi]," *Hokkaido Daigaku Daigaku-bunsho-kan Nenpo* (Annual Report of Hokkaido University Archives), no. 12, pp. 53–67.

Yamanishi, Tei (2007), "Tsujimura Michiyo, Japan's First Doctor of Agriculture in Tea Research," in Iwao and Hara (eds.) 2007, pp. 23–29.

Yamashita, Aiko (ed.) (1983), *Kindai nihon joseishi: Kagaku* [History of Modern Japanese Women: Science], Tokyo: Kajima Shuppankai.

Yamazaki, Takako (1962), *Tsuda Umeko*, Tokyo: Yoshikawa Kobunkan.

Yasui, Kono (1905), "Koi no weberu-shi kikan ni tuite [On the Organ of Mr. Uebel in Carp]," *Dobutsugaku Zasshi* (Zoological Journal), vol. 17, no. 201, pp. 207–211.

Yasui, Kono (1911), "On the Life-history of Salvia natans," *Annals of Botany*, vol. 25, pp. 469–484.

Yatsu, Naohide (1939), "Kenkyu-shitsu gaikan: Tokyo Teikoku Daigaku Rigakubu Dobutsugaku Kyositsu no rekishi [Laboratory Overview: History of the Department of Zoology, Faculty of Science, Tokyo Imperial University] (1)," *Kagaku* (Science), vol. 8, pp. 340–246, (2) pp. 387–389, (3) pp. 435–438.

Yomiuri Shimbun (1921), "Shokuhin-kagaku no kenkyu ni Tange joshi ga tobei [Ms. Tange goes to the U.S. to study food chemistry]," March 5.

Yomiuri Shimbun (1943), "Tatakau kagaku no bunya ni josei no shinshutu ichijirushi, RIKEN kenkyu happyo ni shin kyochi wo hiraku [Women's Advancement in the Field of Wartime Science Opens New Horizons in Research Presentations at RIKEN]," June 15.

Yonezawa, Fumiko (2009), *Saruhashi Katuko toiu ikikata* [The Way of Life of Saruhashi Katsuko], Tokyo: Iwanami Shoten.

Yoshikawa, Toshikazu (1930), *Tsuda Umeko*, Tokyo: Fujin Shimbun.

Yoshikawa, Toshikazu (1956), *Tsuda Umeko den* [Biography of Tsuda Umeko], a revised edition of Yoshikawa 1930, *Tsuda Umeko*, Tokyo: Tsuda Juku Doso-kai.

Yoshikawa, Toshikazu (1990), *Tsuda Umeko*, a pocket book edition with an annotation of Yoshikawa 1930, Tokyo: Chuko Bunko.

Yoshimura Akashiko wo shinobu kai (Group to Commemorate Yoshimura Akashiko) (ed.) (1980), *Subete no kotomo ni kagaku wo: Yoshimura Akashiko wo kataru* [Science All Children: Talking about Yoshimura Akashiko], Tokyo: Yoshimura Akashiko wo Shinobu Kai.

Yoshimura, Akashiko (1969, 1970, 1971), "Nihon ni okeru josei kagakusha no ayumi to sono haikei [The Trajectories of Women Scientists in Japan and Their Backgrounds]," *Tsuda Juku Daigaku Kiyo* (Bulletin of Tsuda College), no.1 (1969), pp. 16–29; (II): no. 2 (1970), pp. 113–126; (III): no. 3 (1971), pp. 169–184.

Yoshimura, Mako (2000), "Yoshimura Akashiko: Subeteno kodomoni kagakuwo: Kagaku yomimono no kenkyu, fukyu, sozou no kusawake toshite [Yoshimura Akashiko: Science to All Children: As a Pioneer in Research, Popularization, and Creation of Science Readings]," in Tsuda Juku Daigaku soritsu 100 shunen kinen-shi shuppan iinkai (ed.) 2000, pp. 70–72.

Yukawa, Tsugiyoshi (2003), *Kindai Nihon no Josei to daigaku kyoiku: Kyoiku kikai Kaiho wo meguru rekishi* [Women and University Education in Modern Japan: A History of Opening Educational Opportunities], Tokyo: Fuji Shuppan.

Map of the Eastern United States

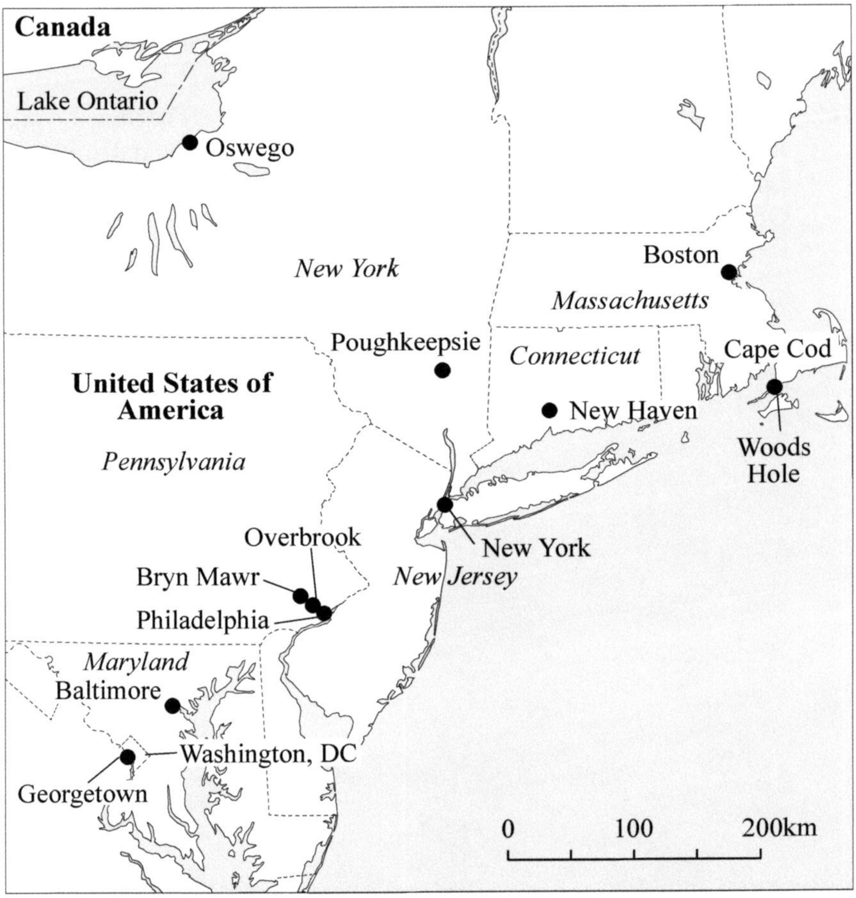

Name Index

Aiya Sakae, 36

Bacon, Alice, 30–32, 38, 84, 101, 110
Beadle, George, 90
Boring, Alice, 163
Brooks, William, 50, 54, 83, 123

Conklin, Edwin, 51, 73
Cooke, Elizabeth, 69

Dan Katsuma, 71
Darwin, Charles, 18, 45
Delbrück, Max, 90

Einstein, Albert, 137–138
Empress Shoken, 35
Evans, Anne, 69

Fujii Kenjiro, 154
Fujita Taki, 117, 135–137
Fukuzawa Yukichi, 14, 17
Furukawa Haruo, 136, 138

Gobara Sawako, 148
Goff, Leah, 55, 77, 83

Harrison, Ross, 51
Hartshorne, Anna, 79, 87, 165
Hashida Kunihiko, 132
Hayashi Masako, 148
Hayashi Taro, 137
Hijikata Hisamoto, 42
Hiratsuka Raicho, 97–98, 109
Holmes, Lulu, 142–143
Hooibrenk, Daniel, 15
Hopkins, Johns, 49
Hoshino Ai, 11, 106–107, 117–127, 131–135, 139–140, 142–143, 147–148, 165–166
Hoshino Yoshiro, 147
Hyde, Ida, 58, 69, 77–79, 163

Ide Hiro, 153
Iijima Isao, 86
Inoue Jinkichi, 132
Ishikawa Chiyomatsu, 85
Ito Hirobumi, 25, 31, 33, 110
Ito Ume, 32
Iwakawa Tomotaro, 88, 154
Iwakura Tomomi, 24
Iwamoto Yoshiharu, 95, 104

Kaji Umetaro, 39–40
Kamichika Ichiko, 109–110
Kaminaka Fumiko, 148
Kanayama Raku, 81
Kanda Naibu, 31, 36
Kanie Misao, 126
Kanno Nobuko, 148
Kasuya Yoshi, 126, 140
Kato Sechi, 151, 153, 160–161
Katsu Kaishu, 40
Kawai Michi, 119–120, 142
Kawamoto Shizuko, 112–113
Kawashima Yoshiko, 125
Keiser, Edward, 57–58
Keller, Ida A., 55, 77

Kido Takayoshi, 25
Kikuchi Dairoku, 95
Komai Taku, 67, 72, 89
Kuroda Chika, 81, 153, 155–156, 161–162
Kuroda Kiyotaka, 21
Kuroda Takao, 136–138
Kuwaki Ayao, 134, 137–138

Lanman, Adeline, 35–37, 45–46, 110
Lanman, Charles, 26–27
Lee, Frederic, 52–53, 55, 57–58, 63
Loeb, Jacques, 55, 58, 77–78

Majima Riko, 158
Martin, Henry, 50
Matsubara Koichi, 134, 137–138
Matsuda Michi, 120
Meiji Emperor, 60
Mendel, Gregor Johann, 89
Mitsuishi Iwao, 136, 139, 147
Mitsukuri Genpachi, 84
Mitsukuri Kakichi, 83–87, 152
Miyakawa Kanoeko, 153
Morgan (*nee* Sampson), Lilian, 89
Morgan, Thomas, 7, 51, 55, 58, 67, 69–77, 79–83, 85–86, 89–90, 124, 152, 163
Mori Arinori, 17, 21, 23, 26
Morris, Mary, 39–40, 54, 82
Morris-Suzuki, Tessa, 16
Morse, Edward, 68, 84–86, 88
Motoda Nagazane, 61
Muller, Hermann, 90

Nagai Nagayoshi, 157–158
Nagai Shigeko, *see* Uryu (*nee* Nagai) Shigeko
Nakagiri Kakutaro, 126
Nakajima Rikizo, 36
Nakamura Chiyomatsu, 102–103
Nakamura Mikae, 153
Nakanishi Fumiko, 5, 80
Nakayama Shigeru, 147
Nakazawa Shingo, 75, 163
Nanbara Shigeru, 142
Naruse Jinzo, 95, 99, 157
Nishida Kitaro, 114
Nishimura Shigeki, 40, 42
Nitobe Inazo, 95, 104, 111, 114, 125
Noguchi Hideyo, 71
Nukada Yutaka, 129–130

Oba Minako, 5, 151
Ogawa Junjiro, 136
Ohashi Hiro, 156, 162
Okajima Masae, 137
Okami Keiko, 53–54
Okubo Toshimichi, 25
Okuma Shigenobu, 97–99
Ono Tomogoro, 14
Ooi Koshiro, 136
Oppenheimer, Jane, 72
Oshima Hiroshi, 68, 73
Osugi Sakae, 109
Otori Keisuke, 42
Oyama Iwao, 32, 110
Oyama (*nee* Yamakawa) Sutematsu/Sutematz, 22–23, 25–33, 38, 40, 47, 50, 59, 84, 87, 96–97, 101, 110–111

Pestalozzi, Johann, 43
Pflüger, Eduard, 75
Powers, Anna, 60
Randolph, Harriet, 123
Rhodes, James, 52
Roux, Wilhelm, 51, 75

Sakui Seita, 147–148
Sakurai Joji, 84
Sampson, Lilian, *see* Morgan (*nee* Sampson), Lilian
Saruhashi Katsuko, 98
Sato Ikuyo, 153
Sato Kimiko, 140, 147–148
Sawayanagi Masataro, 160
Scott, Charlotte, 121
Sedgwick, William, 55
Senju Katsumi, 61
Shimoda Utako, 31, 33–34, 99
Shimokobe Chiho, 148
Siebold, Philipp Franz von, 15, 138
Stevens, Nettie, 123–124
Sugai Junichi, 136, 138
Suzuki Hideru, 156, 162
Suzuki Umetaro, 158–159, 162
Suzuki Utako, 120

Takahashi Yuko, 2, 21
Takamine Hideo, 43, 84, 95
Takehara Kumakichi, 134, 136
Takenaka Haruko, 148
Takeuchi Shigeyo, 153
Tamson, Ruth Ray, 126
Tange Ume, 81, 156–157, 159, 161–162
Taylor, Joseph, 47, 49, 53
Tennent, David, 123
Terasaka Yumi, 26
Thomas, Martha Carey, 47–49, 55, 59, 79–81, 90, 100, 121
Toda Kuni, 153
Tolstoy, 107
Tsuda Fukiko, 13–14, 35
Tsuda Gingo, 13–14
Tsuda Hatsuko, 13, 14, 35, 110
Tsuda Jiro, 13, 35
Tsuda Jun, 14, 35
Tsuda Kingo, 13–14
Tsuda Kiyoko, 14, 35
Tsuda Kotoko, 13–14, 24, 35, 110
Tsuda Mariko, 14, 35
Tsuda Motochika, 13–14, 35
Tsuda Sen, 10, 13–21, 24, 35–36, 39–40, 57, 82, 90, 95, 104, 110
Tsuda Tomiko, 14, 35
Tsuda Umeko, 1–2, 5–11, 13–16, 20–22, 24–28, 30–43, 45–50, 53, 55–64, 67–91, 93–94, 97, 99–105, 107–114, 117–118, 120–122, 124–127, 133, 140–141, 143, 147–149, 151–152, 155–157, 159, 161–166
Tsuda Yonako, 14, 35
Tsugawa Akiko, 151
Tsuji Matsu, 111–112, 126–127
Tsujimura Michiyo, 36, 153, 155–156, 162

Ueda Teiko, 22, 25
Ueno Eizaburo, 35, 110
Ueno Kotoko, *see* Tsuda Kotoko

Uryu (*nee* Nagai) Shigeko, 22, 25–28, 32, 47, 50, 87, 101, 114
Uryu Sotokichi, 32

Wagener, Gottfried, 17
Warren, Joseph, 55, 58, 77, 122
Watanabe Yoko, 162
Watase Shozaburo, 69, 71–72, 84
Whitman, Charles, 68–69, 84–88
Whitney, Clara, 39–40
Whitney, William, 39
Wilson, Edmund, 51–55, 57–58, 63, 70, 72, 84, 86

Yamada Koto, 114, 126
Yamakawa Hiroshi, 23
Yamakawa Hitoshi, 114
Yamakawa Kenjiro, 23, 96–97
Yamakawa Kikue, 2, 104–105, 107–109, 114
Yamakawa Matsue, 108
Yamakawa Sutematsu, *see* Oyama (Yamakawa) Sutematsu
Yamazaki Saburo, 136
Yasui Kono, 74, 80, 88, 153–155, 161–162
Yasui Tetsu, 99
Yatsu Naohide, 86
Yonezawa Fumiko, 93
Yoshihara Ryu, 153
Yoshikawa Toshikazu, 8, 38, 46, 57, 67, 80, 88–89, 107, 109, 126, 165
Yoshimasu Ryoko, 22, 25
Yoshimura Akashiko, 145–147
Yoshioka Yayoi, 97
Yukawa Hideki, 98

Subject Index

agricultural chemistry, 155
agricultural improvement movement, 19
agriculture, 14–15, 18–19, 146, 153, 159
algebra, 27, 136
American Women's Scholarship for Japanese Women, 82, 119, 120
Amherst College, 36
anarchist, 109
ancient history, 57, 58
Annals of Botany, 74
Anti-Prostitution Law, 110
Aoyama Gakuin, 20
Aoyama Women's School, 128
application for resignation (*jishoku negai-sho*), 40
application to study abroad, 41–42, 62, 64
Arabic, 30
Archer Institute, 27, 30, 57
arithmetic, 27
arts, 27
Ashio Copper Mine, 19
astronomy, 27, 147
Attic Letters (*The*-), 9, 37
Austria, 15

Baika Women's Vocational School, 128
Baltimore, 49
Barnard College, 47
Bible, 112, 118, 124
Bikai Seminary, 20
biology, 1, 7–11, 43, 46, 50–52, 54, 56–59, 63–65, 67–68, 71, 73, 76–77, 79–84, 87–91, 105, 113, 117, 119, 122–125, 128, 130, 133, 136, 146, 152, 154, 161–162, 164–165
  department of -, 46, 50–53, 55–57, 59, 71, 76–77, 83–84, 86, 88, 122
Blue Stockings Society (*Seito-sha*), 98, 109
bookkeeping, 125
Boshin War, 23
Boston, 68, 125
  Women's Education Association of-, 68
botany, 29, 55, 70, 86, 119, 123, 154, 156
British history, 124
Bryn Mawr College, 2, 7, 10, 40, 42–43, 45–56, 58–60, 63–64, 67, 69–70, 72–75, 77–80, 83, 88, 90–91, 100, 113, 118–123, 136, 163–164
  -Program, 56
Bushido, 104

California Institute of Technology, 72, 80
Chemical Society of Japan, 137
chemistry, 8, 29, 50, 56, 60–61, 81, 122, 125, 128, 130, 133–134, 137, 143–144, 146, 155, 157–160, 166
  department of -, 143
Chinese classics, 103, 119
Christianity, 19, 23, 26

chromosome, 89–90, 123
Clark University, 52, 68, 71
Columbia University, 52, 55, 72–73, 80, 86, 89, 108, 126, 142, 163
Committee of Seven to Appeal for World Peace (World Peace 7), 98
comparative anatomy, 56–58, 63
Cornell University, 77
cytology, 54

Dalton Hall, 83
Dampatsu Rei, 15
department of foreign languages, 135
department of home economics, 125, 130, 132, 146
Department of Practical Training (*Jisshu-ka*), 125
development, 51, 72, 75, 83,
 developmental mechanics, 51
Dobutsu shinka-ron [Animal Evolution Theory], 85
Dobutsugaku Zasshi (Zoological Journal), 87
domestic feminism, 99
domestic science, *see* home economics
domesticity, 22, 48
Doshisha Women's School (Senmon-bu), 120, 128
Drexel University, 54
Drosophila, 89, 163

economics, 136
Effects of Other Fertilization and Self-Fertilization in Plants (*The-*), 18
elementary school (*jinjo shogakko*), 94
elocution, 122
embryology, 72, 80, 86, 89, 163
Emergency Wartime Measures Concerning Education, 129
English department, 128, 131, 144
English literature, 58, 108, 113, 128, 131, 143
 history of -, 122
ethics, 58, 103–104, 126
evolutionary theory, 51, 85
experimental embryology, 51, 72, 75–76, 86, 90
experimental zoology, 51

Faculty of Liberal Arts, 144, 146
female scientists, 3, 11, 78, 98, 117, 136, 151–154, 161–162, 164
feminist, 48, 90–91, 100
Ferris Waei Girls' School, 118
first generation of women in higher education, 47
first-wave feminism, 48
food science, 161
French, 27, 29, 50
frog, 5, 74–76, 82, 85–86, 124, 152
Fukuoka Prefectural Women's Vocational School, 128, 130

Gakunosha Agricultural School, 17, 19–20, 35, 39
Gakushuin, 33, 36
 - Archives, 2, 27, 40–42, 64, 82
Genshi, josei wa taiyo de atta [Originally, Women Were the Sun], 97

gender, 1, 6, 9–10, 21, 34, 48, 90, 95, 145, 161, 164–165
gene, 89–90
general biology, 52, 54, 56–58, 77
General Headquarters of the Allied Forces, 142
general zoology, 57–58
genetics, 72, 80, 89–90, 154
geography, 27
geology, 29
geology and mineralogy, 134
(sub-departments) of -, 133,
geometry, 27, 121
Georgetown, 26, 28
German, 29, 45, 50, 122
gibbous beetles, 72
Gifu, 154
Girls' Elementary School, 20
girls' high school (*koto jogakko*), 94–95, 154
good wife and wise mother (*ryosai kenbo*), 21, 30, 34, 48, 95, 99–100, 157
- principle, 106
government-financed/funded study abroad, 22, 45
government-sponsored student, 21, 81
Great Kanto Earthquake, 103, 114, 123, 126
Greek, 46, 50
gymnastics, 103

Harvard University, 48, 62, 154
Hayama Hikage Chaya incident, 110
health, 52
Heibonsha, 147
high school (*koto gakko*), 94
Higher Normal School, 23, 134
Hinomaru, 19
Hirosaki, 109
Hiroshima Prefectural Women's Vocational School, 130
histology, 55–56, 58
history (study), 27, 29, 56–57, 84, 103, 119–120, 136, 142–143
history and political economy, 50
history of linguistics, 124
history of religion, 50
History of Science Society of Japan, 6, 138
Hitachi Aircraft, 139
Hokkaido Imperial University, 160
Hokkaido *Kaitakushi* (Hokkaido Development Commission), 21, 23
home economics, 48, 125, 128, 157
- movement, 48
horticultural lectures, 15
housework, 48, 161
hygiene, 125

Imperial Household Agency's Archives, 40
Imperial Instructions (*goshinyu*), 60, 61
imperial universities (*teikoku daigaku*), 81, 83, 155
Imperial Women's Medical and Pharmaceutical Vocational School, 129, 145
Imperial Women's Medical Vocational School, 128
Imperial Women's Vocational School, 128

Imperial Women's Vocational School of Pharmacy, 128
Imperial Women's Vocational School of Science, 130, 134, 145
Inamuragasaki, 114
inorganic chemistry, 57–58
Institute for Physical and Chemical Research, *see* RIKEN
Instructions for Western Travels (*Yoko Kokoroe-sho*), 26
Italian, 50
Iwakura Mission (Iwakura Shisetsudan), 22, 24, 32

Japan Association of Women's Education, 95
Japan Socialist Party, 110
Japan Women's University, 97–99, 128–130, 143, 146, 153, 156–159
Japan Women's Vocational School of Dental Medicine, 128
Japanese (study), 103, 119, 135
Japanese literature, 128, 132, 143
Jikei Hospital, 54
Jissen Girls' School, 99
Jissen Women's Vocational School, 128
Jogaku Zasshi, 74–75, 104
Johns Hopkins University, 49–50, 52, 55–56, 72, 83–84, 123, 152, 158–159
Joshi Eigaku Juku (Women's School for English Studies), 5, 8, 11, 48, 87–89, 93–94, 97, 100–105, 108, 110–111, 114, 119–120, 124–126, 136, 148, 164–165
Joshi Gakushuin, 34
junior high school (*chugakko*), 94

Kagaku Chishiki (Scientific Knowledge), 152
Kagakusi Kenkyu (Study of the History of Science), 138
Kamakura, 109–110, 114
Kanda Christian Youth Association, 19
Kassui Women's Vocational School, 128
kazoku, 33
Keisen Girls' School, 120
Kobe College, 142–143
Kobe College Vocational School, 128
Kochi Prefectural Women's Vocational School, 130
Koishikawa Botanical Garden, 154
Koka Women's Vocational School, 130
Kokyo School, 20
Kosetsu Chemistry Hall, 157–158
Kyoritsu Women's Vocational School, 128
Kyoto Imperial University, 95–96, 135
Kyoto Prefectural Women's Vocational School, 130
Kyoto University, 73
Kyoto Women's Vocational School, 128
Kyushu Imperial University, 96, 134, 137–138

laboratory work, 56–58, 63, 122, 141, 158
Latin, 27, 29, 46, 50

letter of instructions (*osata-sho*), 24
liberal arts, 29, 50, 57, 99, 121, 130, 134, 144
literary criticism, 29
literature, 27
logic, 27, 29, 58

major (courses), 56–58, 77, 123–124
mathematics, 27, 29, 50, 57, 81, 93, 119–121, 128–130, 133, 135, 138, 143–145, 166
  department of -, 121, 129, 135, 143–144, 146
medicine, 22, 52, 152–153
Meiji Girl's School, 104
Meiroku Zasshi, 17
Meirokusha, 17
mentor, 1, 100, 152–154, 156, 158–159, 163
Merrion Hall, 60
metallurgical engineering, 148
Methodist, 19
microscope, 70, 84, 134
mineralogy, 29
Ministry of Education, 32–33, 106, 129–131, 133–134, 136, 142–143, 154, 157–158, 161
  Radio Physics Research Institute, 139
Ministry of Home Affairs, 19, 158
Ministry of the Imperial Household, 33
minor (courses), 56–58, 63, 77, 122
Misaki Marine Biological Station, 84, 123, 152
Miyagi Prefectural Women's Vocational School, 128, 130
mobilized to work, 139
morality, 104
morphology, 56, 71, 86
Mount Holyoke College, 37, 46, 163
music, 27, 32, 87
mutation, 72, 89, 163

Nara Women's Higher Normal School, 93, 146
Nara Women's University, 93, 146
natural history, 27
natural science, 6, 11, 50, 57, 61, 74, 91, 117, 133, 144, 152–153, 157, 161, 164–165
New Haven, 23
  New Haven Hospital, 29
New York, 27, 42–43, 68, 104, 126
  - State University, Oswego, 62
Nihon University, 136
Nobel Prize, 71, 89–90
  in Physiology or Medicine, 55, 72, 89, 163
Nogyo Sanji (Three Processes in Agriculture), 15–18
Nogyo Zasshi (Agricultural Journal), 17, 19
normal school, 37, 117, 136
Numata Elementary School, 118
Numazu, 111
nursing, 29
nutritional chemistry, 156, 158, 161–162

Ochanomizu University, 2, 145–146, 155
Okayama Seishin Women's Vocational School, 130
On the Origin of Species, 18

organic chemistry, 161
Orientation of the Frog's Egg (The-), 74, 76
Osaka Prefectural Women's Vocational School, 128, 130
Osaka University, 148
Oswego Normal School, 42–43, 62
Otani Women's Vocational School, 130
Overbrook, 40
Oxford University, 161

Pacific War, 127, 129, 131, 151
patriarchal system, 36, 100, 165
pedagogy, 42, 126
Peeresses' School, 7, 11, 27, 30, 33–35, 38, 40, 42, 60, 63–64, 81–82, 90, 164
pharmacy, 156
Philadelphia, 1, 6–7, 40, 42, 47
  World's Fair, 28
philosophy, 10, 19, 29, 46–47, 49–50, 56, 58, 122, 132, 157
physical chemistry, 160
physics, 23, 27, 29, 50, 56, 122, 128, 130, 133, 136, 144, 146, 166
  - department, 143
physiology, 27, 30, 32, 52, 56, 58, 78, 88, 90, 123–125, 134, 136
pollination, 17–19
  - aid method controversy, 17
population studies, 125
post-major (courses), 56, 58, 73, 124
Poughkeepsie, 27
practical training department, 132
prohibition of alcohol, 19
prohibition of Christianity (*takafuda tekkyo* or removal of notice board), 26
promote university for women, 142
prosopography, 162
Protestant/ -ism, 19, 26
psychology, 27, 58, 103, 122
Puritan, 19

Quaker, 39–40, 47–49
qualification for the non-examination of secondary school teachers, 102
Quarterly Journal of Microscopical Science, 74

Radcliffe College, 46
Radio Physics Research Institute, 139
Regulations for Studying Abroad (*kaigai ryugaku kisoku*), 22
research universities, 49
reverse culture shock, 34
rhetoric, 29
RIKEN, 156, 159–162
RIKEN Bulletin (*RIKEN Iho*), 159
Rockefeller Institute, 71
Rokumeikan, 32
role model, 24, 30, 39, 154, 156, 159, 163
Russo-Japanese War, 106

Sacred Heart Women's Higher Vocational School, 128
San Francisco, 15, 25, 30

science, 1, 6–7, 9–11, 16, 20, 22, 29, 38, 45, 57, 59–61, 72, 80, 87–88, 90, 100, 117, 120, 122, 124, 128–130, 132–134, 136–141, 143–147, 151–156, 160–162, 164–165
- education, 10, 87–88, 124, 129–130, 147, 153, 165
history of -, 1, 3, 9–10, 138–139, 146–147, 164
science department [Rika], 50, 87, 117–118, 124, 127–128, 131, 133–139, 141, 144, 147–148
Scientific Papers, 159
sea urchins, 72
secondary teaching certification exam, 157
segregation (*sumiwake*), 144, 161–162
Seijo High School, 136
Seito (Blue Stockings), 98
Seven Sisters, 46–47
sewing, 61
Sheffield Scientific School, 23
Shizuoka Eiwa School, 120
Shoei Girls' School, 54
Shoin Women's Vocational School, 128, 130
sideline student, 157
Simmons College, 125
Small Flock of Disciples (*chiisaki deshi no mure*), 120
Smith College, 37, 46, 73
snake venom, 71
Society of Industrial Chemistry, 132
Society of Japanese Women Scientists, 98
Spanish, 50
Spanish flu, 111
Special School, 20
special student, 46, 77, 124, 163
St. Luke's Hospital, 112
starfish, 72
State University of New York, Oswego, 2, 62
Stephenson Seminary, 26–27
study abroad application, 40
Supreme Commander of the Allied Powers, 142
Suzumine Women's Vocational School, 130

taxonomy, 86
Taylor Hall, 53–54
Teachers College, 126
teaching methods, 42–43, 62
technology translation, 16
theory of national ruin caused by women doctors (*joi bokoku-ron*), 97
theory of relativity, 137
three processes of agriculture, 16
Toho University, 2, 145
Tohoku Imperial University, 81, 132, 157, 160
Tokyo Academy of Music, 32
Tokyo Academy of Physics, 136–137
Tokyo Bunrika University, 137
Tokyo Eiwa School, 20
Tokyo English School, 20
Tokyo Girls' High School, 32
Tokyo Higher Normal School, 36, 43, 136

Tokyo Imperial University, 23, 36, 71, 80, 95–96, 123, 134, 136, 142, 154–155, 157, 159

Tokyo Institute of Technology, 148

Tokyo Prefectural Women's Vocational School, 130

Tokyo Society of Biology, 87

Tokyo University of Science, 137

Tokyo Woman's Christian University, 99, 104, 128–129, 143

Tokyo Women's Higher Normal School, 32, 137, 146, 153–155, 160

Tokyo Women's Medical School, 97

Tokyo Women's Medical University, 97

Tokyo Women's Medical Vocational School, 128

Tokyo Women's Normal School, 32

Tokyo Women's Theological Vocational School, 128

Tokyo Women's Vocational School, 128

Tokyo Zoological Society, 85, 87

Toyo Gakugei Zasshi, 86

Toyo Girls' School, 34

Toyo Women's Vocational School of Dental Medicine, 128

trigonometry, 27, 121

Tsuda College, 11, 118, 126–127, 135–136, 139, 143–144, 146–148, 166

Tsuda Eigaku Juku, 111, 117, 127, 131–132, 134, 148

Tsuda Juku Senmon Gakko (Tsuda Juku Vocational School), 130, 134, 146–148

Tsuda Juku's Science Department, 136, 145

Tsuda nawa, 17–19

Tsuda Umeko bunsho [The Writings of Tsuda Umeko], 9

Tsuda University, 5, 8–9, 162, 164

- Archives, 2, 9, 16, 25, 28, 31, 37, 58–59, 76, 78, 82–83, 85, 101–103, 113, 126–127, 140–141, 147

United States Education Mission to Japan, 142

University of California, 55

University of Chicago, 52, 55, 71, 154

University of Electro-Communications, 148

University of Heidelberg, 78

University of Kansas, 78, 163

University of Pennsylvania, 6

University of the Sacred Heart, 143

University of Tokyo, 3, 23, 68, 84–86, 88, 146–148

- Society of Biology, 86

University of Tsukuba School for the Blind, 20

University Ordinance (*Daigaku Rei*), 129

Vassar College, 2, 27, 29–32, 46, 50, 59, 84

Victorian era, 21, 26, 100

Victorian view of the family, 48, 100

Vienna Exposition/World Exposition, 15, 18

vitamin B_2, 159

vocational school (*senmon gakko*), 94, 98–99, 101–103, 128–130, 132, 137, 142, 145–146, 154, 156

Vocational School Ordinance (*Senmon Gakko Rei*), 101, 125, 129

Washington, DC, 26, 28, 59

Wellesley College, 37, 46, 62

wise mother, *see* good wife and wise mother

Woman's Medical College of Pennsylvania, 52

Women and Youth Bureau of the Ministry of Labor, 105

women scientists, *see* female scientists

women's education, 33, 64, 79, 95, 106, 128, 142, 144–145

women's higher education, 11, 82, 99–100

  superfluous/disadvantageous/ arguments against-/ hostile to-, 11, 95–96, 100

  theory that_ is harmful, 97

women's higher normal schools (*joshi koto shihan gakko*), 94, 128, 142, 154

women's history, 8, 26

women's normal school (*joshi shihan gakko*), 30, 94

women's universities, 142–143, 145, 166

Women's University League (Joshi Daigaku Renmei) , 142

Women's Vocational School of Economics, 130

Woods Hole Marine Biological Laboratory, 2, 68–71, 73–74

World War II, 34, 94, 118, 153

Yale College, 23, 36

Yale University, 83

zoology, 29, 32, 56, 69, 84–89, 119, 152